Cooking With Chloe

CHLOE & JAY SUTLIFFE

TEACH Services, Inc.
PUBLISHING
www.TEACHServices.com • (800) 367-1844

World rights reserved. This book or any portion thereof may not be copied or reproduced in any form or manner whatever, except as provided by law, without the written permission of the publisher, except by a reviewer who may quote brief passages in a review.

The author assumes full responsibility for the accuracy of all facts and quotations as cited in this book. The opinions expressed in this book are the author's personal views and interpretations, and do not necessarily reflect those of the publisher.

This book is provided with the understanding that the publisher is not engaged in giving spiritual, legal, medical, or other professional advice. If authoritative advice is needed, the reader should seek the counsel of a competent professional.

Copyright © 2017 Chloe & Jay Sutliffe

Copyright © 2017 TEACH Services, Inc.

ISBN-13: 978-1-4796-0783-9 (Paperback)

ISBN-13: 978-1-4796-0784-6 (ePub)

Library of Congress Control Number: 2017909659

Introduction

This collection of recipes has been a project that I come back to year after year. When Jay and I opened "The Garden" in Grand Forks, ND (1993-1997) I began tweaking recipes to suit our taste and the taste of our customers. During the years we spent at "Veggies" in Rapid City, SD (2001-2005) more recipes were added to the collection. The majority of the recipes in this book are a result of our years at Veggies. Each of these recipes is truly restaurant tested and so well received that I wanted to share them with others.

I am so thankful for all the customers of both restaurants who tasted each of these recipes and came back for more. A thank you goes to all of my friends who helped work through this project with me and all the sage advice that they have given. It is my hope and desire that you will benefit—mentally, socially, physically, and spiritually as a result of the information compiled in this cookbook.

Sincerely;

Chloe A. Sutliffe

A Special Note

All the temperatures in this book are in Fahrenheit and all herb measurements are for dry herbs unless otherwise specified.

Table of Contents

Start Your Day with Breakfast 7

Special Breads 19

Savory Main Dishes 29

Spreads, Gravies & Miscellaneous 55

Seasonings 63

Sides 67

Salads 77

Soups 95

Sweets (Desserts) 103

Index 121

Start Your Day with Breakfast

Fresh Whole Fruit

Begin your breakfast with fresh whole fruit such as apples, pears, plums, apricots, strawberries, cherries, peaches, blueberries, oranges, melons, bananas, pineapple, avocados, etc. Fruits are great natural cleansers, which help the body detoxify. They are nutritious and easy to digest. So start your day with a generous amount of fresh fruit.

If eating fresh whole fruit is not appealing to you, try cutting some up and arranging it on a platter. Cut the top off of a pineapple, and place it in the middle of your platter. Cut in bite sized pieces equal parts of papaya, pineapple, and mango. This is so refreshing and delightfully delicious. You may use orange sections in place of or along with mango.

If fresh fruit is not available, frozen is next best.

Crunchy Granola

3½ cups **oatmeal**
½ cup **sunflower seeds**
½ cup **coconut**
½ tablespoon **rice flour**
¼ cup **chopped nuts**
¼ cup **sesame seeds**
1 cup **dates**
1 tablespoon **vanilla**
1 teaspoon **salt**

Mix together in a bowl the oatmeal, sunflower seeds, coconut, rice flour, and chopped nuts. Set aside.

Blend together in a blender the sesame seeds, dates, vanilla, salt, and 1 ½ cups warm water.

Mix both sets of ingredients together. Divide mixture in half, spread on cookie sheets.

Bake for 3–4 hours at 200 degrees. Make sure the granola is completely dry. Cool and store in airtight container.

MAKES: 5 cups

Honey Granola

1 cup **honey**
⅓ cup **oil** (optional)
½ cup **pitted dates**
2 teaspoons **salt**
1 tablespoon **vanilla**

12 cups **rolled oats (old fashioned)**
1 cup **hot water**
½ cup **wheat germ**
½ cup **sesame seeds**
1 cup **sunflower seeds & walnuts**

Blend honey, oil, dates, salt, vanilla and hot water together.

Mix oats, wheat germ, sesame seeds, sunflower seeds, and walnuts together in a large bowl.

Pour honey mixture over oat mixture. Mix together. You may find that your hands work best.

Divide into two pans and bake in a 250-degree oven.

Bake for 1½ hours or until dried out, stirring occasionally.

MAKES: 14 cups

> **Tips/Comments**
> If desired you may add 2 cups of raisins (or other dried fruit) after the oats are baked.

Whole Wheat Crepes

2 cups **nut milk, soy milk, or water**
1 teaspoon **vanilla**
2 tablespoons **cornstarch**
1¼ cup **whole wheat pastry flour**
½ teaspoon **salt**

Blend together in a blender the liquid, vanilla, cornstarch, flour, and salt together until they are smooth.

Pour ¼–⅓ cup into heated and sprayed skillet.

Swirl the mixture around the pan, cooking on medium heat until crepe changes color. Turn crepe and cook for 2 more minutes on that side.

MAKES: 10 crepes

Almond Milk

1 cup **almonds, soaked**
2 teaspoons **honey or a few dates**
½ teaspoon **vanilla** (optional)
Pinch of **salt**

Soak almonds overnight in water.

Rinse well.

Blend in a blender with 1 or 2 cups water.

Pour into a cheesecloth and milk out liquid.

Return to blender and add honey or dates, vanilla, and salt with water to make a total of 1 quart.

Smoothies

2 cups **soy, almond or rice milk, or fruit juice**
3 frozen **bananas**
1 cup **frozen fruit (your choice)**

Blend liquids, bananas, and fruit until everything is smooth.

SERVES: 2

Basic Bagel Recipe

Step 1

3 cups **warm water** (110–120 degrees)
¼ cup **apple juice concentrate or honey**
1 tablespoon + 1 teaspoon **yeast**
4–5 cups **whole wheat flour**
2 teaspoons **salt**
2½ cups **unbleached white flour**

Place water, sweetener, and yeast in a mixing bowl. Stir together until yeast is dissolved, and let rise for 5 minutes.

Add salt and flour to make a stiff dough, not sticky to touch. This dough will be stiffer than regular bread dough. You want it to be stiff enough not to stick to your hands when you're working it into bagel shapes.

Add fruit and or nuts for variety.

Divide dough into 12–15 equal parts. Take one part and roll it into a long strip 6–7 inches long. Take ends and pinch together tightly so as to form a circle.

Place each bagel on a lightly sprayed cookie sheet; you should be able to get six on each sheet because you don't want them to touch as they rise. When all bagels are done, place cookie sheets in the refrigerator overnight. Do not cover.

Step 2

Bring a large pan of water to a good boil and boil each bagel for about 30 seconds on each side. Put back onto cookie sheets.

Bake at 425 degrees for about 12 minutes.

MAKES: 12 to 15 bagels

> **Tips/Comments**
>
> Note: The slow proof of the overnight rise in the refrigerator is important in the production of bagels. When they rise slowly, they are less likely to shrink when done baking. As they set in the refrigerator, they dry out a little on the outside, giving them that chewy outside layer.

Berry Crunch

1 cup **fresh or frozen raspberries, unsweetened**
1½ cups **fresh or frozen blueberries, unsweetened**
1½ cups **fresh or frozen pitted cherries, unsweetened**
3½ to 4 tablespoons **cornstarch**
¼ cup **juice concentrate**

Stir juice concentrate with cornstarch and mix together with the fruit (if using frozen fruit, thaw first).

Topping:

1 cup **rolled oats**
3 tablespoons **honey**
3 tablespoons **whole wheat flour**
2 tablespoons **oil**
1 teaspoon **coriander**
2 tablespoons **orange or apple juice**

Mix oats, honey, flour, oil, coriander, and juice together well, to make a crumbly topping.

Spray an 8x12-inch pan.

Place berries in the bottom of the pan and distribute topping evenly over them.

Bake in a 350-degree oven for 30–35 minutes. Serve warm or cold.

SERVES: 6

Flaky Wheat-Oat Crust

1 cup **oat flour**, slightly packed
1 cup **whole wheat flour**, slightly packed
½ teaspoon **salt**
½ cup **water**
½ cup **canola oil**

> **Tips/Comments**
> For a new look and taste, roll sliced almonds into your crust before baking.

Place flours and salt in a bowl.

Whisk oil and water together to emulsify them. Add to dry ingredients.

Mix together until moist and roll out for the type of crust you desire. If baked alone, prick with fork and bake at 350 degrees for 25 minutes. This recipe makes two 9-inch pie crusts.

California Tofu

1¼ pounds **extra firm tofu**, cut into cubes
1 tablespoon **onion powder**
2 tablespoons **nutritional yeast flakes**
1 tablespoon **Chicken-style Seasoning** (p. 64)
1 teaspoon **parsley**
½ teaspoon **basil**
⅛ teaspoon **paprika**
⅛ teaspoon **turmeric**

Place cubed tofu on a sprayed baking sheet.

Blend seasonings with ¼ cup water and pour over tofu.

Bake in a 350-degree oven until slightly browned. Or you may mix together and sauté in a small amount of oil to blend flavors. Serve like scrambled eggs.

SERVES: 4

Creamy Sweet Schmear

2 cups **warm water**
1 teaspoon **agar-agar powder**
1½ cups **cashews, raw**
¼ cup **maple syrup**
½ teaspoon **clear vanilla**
½ tablespoon **lemon juice**
½ teaspoon **salt**

Dissolve the agar powder in warm water. (It is important to use agar powder verse agar flakes as cooking times vary.)

Place in a saucepan and bring to a boil.

Cover and simmer on low for 4–5 minutes. Once the water/agar mixture has boiled the correct amount of time, transfer to a blender and add cashews.

Blend on high for 1–2 minutes. Add the maple syrup, vanilla, lemon juice, and salt to the cashew/agar mixture and blend well. You may add 1 more tablespoon of maple syrup for added sweetness.

Pour into a mold and chill. Store your Creamy Sweet Schmear in an airtight container for use over the next week.

MAKES: 3 cups

Apple Glaze

3 tablespoons **cornstarch**
1 cup **cold water**
1½ cups **concentrated apple juice**

Mix water and cornstarch together until cornstarch is dissolved. Add juice concentrate.

Heat in a small saucepan until mixture thickens.

Use over fruit for a tasty glaze, for the filling of a pie or over fruit pizza.

MAKES: 2½ cups

> **Tips/Comments**
> You may substitute white grape juice concentrate for apple juice for a distinctly different flavor.

Fruit Pizza

Make Flaky Wheat–Oat Crust (p. 12) or crust of your choice, roll into a flat disk shape, prick with a fork to keep from bubbling.

Bake for 25 minutes at 350 degrees.

Spread cooled crust with Creamy Sweet Smear or use a cream cheese substitute.

Cut and place the desired fruit around the crust, such as strawberries, mandarin oranges, bananas, kiwi, etc. A very pretty design is strawberry halves with a mandarin orange slice between each around the outer edge. Next to the strawberry ring, make a ring of ¼-inch thick banana slices. Next form a ring of kiwi slices, then fill the center in with remaining fruit. Top with Apple Glaze, allow to set, then serve.

SERVES: 8

Creamy Sweet Topping

½ cup **dried pineapple or dried papaya**
½ cup **water**
1 cup **cashews**
1 teaspoon **vanilla**
⅛ teaspoon **salt**

Simmer the dried fruit in water until softened.

Place in a blender and blend until smooth. Add the cashews, vanilla, and salt, blend using just enough hot water to make a heavy cream, about ¾–1 cup water.

This will thicken as it cools. Use as a sweet cream topping. Or make layers of Creamy Sweet Topping, Granola (p. 8), and frozen fruit in a parfait glass for a delicious Fruit Delight. You'll love it!

MAKES: 2¼ cups

Banana French Toast

1¼ cups **rolled oats**
1 ripe **banana**
½ cup **raw cashews**
½ cup **dates**
¼ cup **orange juice**
2 cups **water or soy milk**

Blend oats, banana, cashews, dates, juice, and water or milk until satiny smooth.

Pour batter into flat-bottomed bowl. Dip whole wheat bread into batter.

Brown on both sides in Pam®-sprayed skillet over medium heat.

Serve with topping of choice.

MAKES: 10 slices

Oat Waffles #1

1⅓ cups **oats**
2⅔ cups **hot water**
1½ tablespoons **oil**
¾ teaspoon **salt**
1 teaspoon **vanilla**
2½ tablespoons **apple juice concentrate or honey**
1 cup **whole wheat flour**

Soak oats and water together.

Add oil, salt, vanilla, juice concentrate, honey, and flour to oat mixture.

Spray hot waffle iron with nonstick spray and fill waffle iron with batter leaving a little room around the edges.

Bake about 7–9 minutes.

MAKES: 4 medium waffles

Hash Brown Waffles

1 medium **raw potato**, shredded
¼ teaspoon **Vege–Sal**®*

Mix potato and salt together.

Press into a preheated, oiled waffle iron, spreading potato evenly.

Bake for 7–8 minutes, until nicely browned (the length may vary depending on the heat of your waffle iron.)

MAKES: 2 hash brown waffles

*Vege–Sal® is an all-purpose vegetized salty seasoning. This product can be found in the seasoning section of your local grocery store or in a health food store.

Tips/Comments

1–2 tablespoons shredded carrots mixed with potato gives added color.

Scrambled Tofu

1 pound **firm tofu**
⅛ teaspoon **paprika**
1 teaspoon **onion powder**
⅛ teaspoon **turmeric**
1 tablespoon **Chicken-style Seasoning** (p. 64)

1 tablespoon **soy sauce**
1 teaspoon **cumin**
Fresh or **dried herbs**, if desired

Crumble or grate tofu in a medium bowl.

Combine paprika, onion powder, turmeric, Chicken-style Seasoning, soy sauce, cumin, and herbs in the bowl. Mix until blended.

Cook in a medium skillet until slightly browned.

SERVES: 4

Tips/Comments

For variation, add any of the following: chopped tomato, olives, sautéed onion, garlic, or/and peppers.

"Berry" Good Jam

4 cups **frozen berries**
¾ cup **dried pineapple or papaya**

Place the frozen berries in a bowl on top of the dried fruit. Let stand overnight.

Blend well in a blender the next morning for a natural jam for toast or bagels.

MAKES: *4 cups*

Whipped Topping

2 teaspoons **agar-agar powder**
½ cup **raw cashews,**
1 can **coconut cream** (13.66 fluid ounces)
½ cup **white grape juice concentrate or honey**

1 tablespoon **canola oil**
1 teaspoon **lemon juice**
1 teaspoon **clear vanilla**
¼ teaspoon **salt**

Dissolve the agar powder in 1 cup of water. (It is important to use agar powder verse agar flakes as cooking times vary.)

Place in a saucepan and bring to a boil. Cover and simmer on low for 4–5 minutes.

Transfer to a blender once the water/agar mixture has boiled the correct amount of time. Add cashews.

Blend on high for 1–2 minutes. Add to the blender the following ingredients: coconut cream, white grape juice concentrate or honey, oil, lemon juice, vanilla, and salt. Blend until very smooth.

Place in a medium size bowl and put in the refrigerator. Allow to set. When the whipped topping is set, whip with an electric mixer for 2–3 minutes. Serve on whatever you would use whipped topping on. You may sweeten more or less to your taste.

MAKES: *3½ cups*

"Poo Butter"

¼–½ cup **peanut butter**, depending on desired peanut butter taste
1 cup **Corn Butter** (p. 59)

Mix the peanut butter with the Corn Butter.

Add 1 tablespoon of sweetener, if desired.

Refrigerate.

MAKES: *1¼ to 1½ cups*

> **Tips/Comments**
> This is a great spread for waffles, muffins, pancakes or toast. Helps spread out the fat in peanut butter as well.

Carob "Hot Fudge" Topping

2 cups **boiling water**
½ teaspoon **salt**
1 cup **raw cashews**
½ teaspoon **coffee substitute powder or granules**
5 tablespoons **carob powder**
2 teaspoons **vanilla**
1¼ cups **pitted dates**

Blend water, salt, cashews, coffee substitute powder, carob powder, vanilla, and dates together in a blender on high for 2–3 minutes, stopping several times to stir contents, making sure lumps blend well.

Pour into saucepan and cook over medium to high heat until it thickens, stirring constantly. Serve hot or cold, very rich and good.

MAKES: 3 cups

Delicious Oatmeal

2½ cups **soy or nut milk**
½ teaspoon **salt**
1 teaspoon **vanilla**
1 cup **dried mixed fruit**, chopped
1½ cups **old-fashioned rolled oats**

Bring milk, salt, vanilla, and fruit to a light boil, then add the oats.

Cook together for desired consistency, about 10 minutes.

SERVES: 4

Breakfast Banana Split

Using a medium ice cream scoop, place three mounds of "Delicious Oatmeal" into a banana split dish or other small serving bowl. Cut a peeled banana lengthwise (dip into unsweetened pineapple juice to prevent browning), place a half on either side of cereal mounds.

Top each mound with thickened fruit or a topping such as "Berry" Good Jam (p. 16), Carob "Hot Fudge" (p. 17), or "Poo Butter" (p. 16). Place a dollop of Whipped Topping (p. 16) on each mound and sprinkle with chopped nuts. This is a great treat for breaking the fast!

SERVES: 1

Super Waffles

1 cup uncooked **millet**
1 teaspoon **vanilla**
1 cup **old-fashioned rolled oats**
¼ cup **coconut**
1 teaspoon **salt**
½ cup **nuts**

Place millet, vanilla, oats, coconut, salt, and nuts in a blender with 2 cups of hot water.

Blend until smooth (about two minutes).

Add 1½–2 cups more water to make the batter a heavy cream consistency.

Place ½–1 cup batter in a well-oiled HOT waffle iron. Cook for 6–7 minutes, depending upon size and the heat of your waffle iron. Serve with desired toppings.

MAKES: 4 large waffles

Oat Waffles #2

1 cup **old fashioned oats**
3 cups **hot water**
1 cup **quick cooking oats**
¼ cup **honey**
½ teaspoon **salt**
1 teaspoon **vanilla**
¼ cup **flax seed ground into flax meal** (You may use chia seed instead of flax)
1 tablespoon **oil**
¾ cup **hot water**
Brown rice **flour**

Mix the oats, honey, salt, vanilla, and hot water in a large bowl.

Blend in a blender ground flax or chia seeds, oil, and ¾ cup hot water to a gelatinous consistency, and mix into your large bowl with oat mixture.

Rinse blender with ¼ cup hot water. Add to your bowl. Add enough brown rice flour for proper consistency for your waffle iron, about 1 cup.

Bake in your waffle iron approximately 9 minutes. If you use gluten free oats, these waffles are gluten free!!!

MAKES: 4 medium waffles

Special Breads

Basic Muffins

Preheat oven to 350 degrees F.

4 cups **whole-wheat pastry flour**
1½ cups **oat flour**
1¾ teaspoons **salt**
½ cup **golden flax meal**
1½ tablespoons **aluminum-free baking powder**

2½ cups **water or milk substitute**
¾ cups **honey**
⅓ cup **oil**
½ cup **applesauce**
1½ teaspoons **vanilla**

Sift flours, salt, flax meal, and baking powder together in a large bowl. You may make your own oat flour by blending rolled oats in a dry blender until they become flour consistency.

Blend water or milk, honey, oil, applesauce, and vanilla together in a blender until smooth.

Pour into dry ingredients and mix until all lumps are gone.

Place muffin mixture in sprayed muffin pan, each muffin compartment a little over half full.

Bake at 350 degrees for 35–40 minutes.

MAKES: 12 large muffins or 18 small muffins

Tips/Comments

Because I don't use applesauce very often, I keep single serving cups on hand so as not to have to open a jar that could go to waste. Another idea is to freeze 1/2 cup servings. You may add 2 cups frozen fruit such as blueberries for fruit muffins if desired.

Almond Butter Carob Chip Muffins

Preheat oven to 350 degrees.

3½ cups **whole-wheat pastry flour**
¼ cup **golden flax meal**
1½ tablespoons **aluminum-free baking powder**
1 teaspoon **salt**
1½ cups **soy milk**
¾ cup **honey**
¼ cup **apple sauce**
½ cup **almond butter**
¼ cup **oil**
1 teaspoon **vanilla**
¾ cup **carob chips**
½ cup **chopped roasted almonds**

Mix flour, flax meal, baking powder, and salt together in a medium mixing bowl.

Place soy milk, honey, applesauce, almond butter, oil, and vanilla in a blender and blend until well combined.

Pour into the mixing bowl with the dry ingredients; mix with a hand blender for 2 minutes.

Add the carob chips and almonds. Fold into the dry ingredients.

Place muffin mixture in sprayed muffin pan, each muffin compartment a little over half full.

Bake at 350 degrees for 32 minutes.

MAKES: 12 large or 18 small muffins

Zucchini Muffins

Preheat oven to 350 degrees.

2 tablespoons **of chia or flax seeds**
⅓ cup **oil**
1⅔ cups **almond, soy, or rice milk**
1 tablespoon **lemon juice**
½ cup **applesauce**
1 tablespoon **vanilla**
1⅓ cup **Sucanat**®
2 cups **grated zucchini**, loosely packed
1 to 1½ cups **walnuts**
1 cup **raisins, optional**
3½ cups **whole wheat pastry flour**
1 tablespoon **aluminum-free baking powder**
1 teaspoon **cinnamon**
1 teaspoon **baking soda**
1 teaspoon **salt**

Grind the seeds. Once the seeds are ground, add ½ cup water and the oil. Add ground seeds, water, and oil to blender and whiz together until foamy.

Pour the foamy seed mixture along with milk, lemon juice, applesauce, vanilla, Sucanat®, zucchini, walnuts, and raisins (if using them) into a large mixing bowl. Whisk all these ingredients together until well combined.

Mix in a separate bowl the flour, baking powder, cinnamon, baking soda, and salt. Once the flour, baking soda and powder, salt, and cinnamon are stirred together, add it to the wet ingredient bowl.

Fold together until flour disappears and ingredients are well melded.

Scoop about ⅓ cup of mixture into each muffin well. Bake at 350 degrees for 30 minutes or until muffins are nicely browned and spring back from the touch.

MAKES: 12 large or 18 small muffins

> **Tips/Comments**
>
> To make Banana Muffins, substitute mashed banana for zucchini.
>
> For carrot muffins, substitute shredded carrots for zucchini. This also makes great cake, but when cooking vegan cake, remember, thin layers cook more evenly. So place a little less than one inch in each pan. It's great to have several layers.

Corn Bread

Preheat oven to 350 degrees.

- 2 cups **cornmeal**
- 2 cups **whole wheat pastry flour**
- 2½ tablespoons **aluminum-free baking powder**
- 1 teaspoon **salt**
- 2 cups **soy milk**
- 3 tablespoons **applesauce or egg substitute** (p. 62)
- ⅓ cup **olive oil**
- 3 tablespoons **honey**
- ½ cup **frozen corn**

Mix together the cornmeal, flour, salt, and baking powder. Make a well in the center.

Add the applesauce or egg substitute, milk, oil, and sweetener together in a blender canister and blend well. After you have blended this for 30 seconds, add the frozen corn. Pulse blender to make corn into smaller pieces but leave some of the corn texture.

Add liquid ingredients to the well in the center of flour mixture, and beat until a smooth batter is formed. Add more soy milk if the mixture is too thick.

Place in a sprayed 8x8-inch pan and bake at 350 degrees for 20–25 minutes. If desired, you may sprinkle more whole corn kernels on the top of your batter before baking, along with a pinch of parsley for color.

MAKES: 15 pieces

Whole Wheat Sweet Rolls

Preheat oven to 350 degrees.

1½ cups **warm water (110–120 degrees)**
1 tablespoon **yeast**
½ cup **apple juice concentrate or honey**
½ cup **unbleached bread flour**

1½ teaspoons **salt**
3 cups **whole wheat flour**
¾ cup each, **pecans and raisins**

Mix in a large bowl warm water, yeast, and apple juice or honey until yeast is dissolved. Let stand until foamy about 10 minutes.

Add half of the flour to yeast mixture and mix well, about 3–5 minutes, allowing the gluten to develop. Mix in the rest of the flour along with the salt. Add up to 1 more cup whole wheat flour, adding slowly to the mixture to take away stickiness.

Knead for 15 minutes by hand or for 5 minutes with a bread mixer. Let the dough be slightly sticky to touch but not sticking to your fingers. Last, add the pecans and raisins and mix in thoroughly.

Remove dough from bowl and place on an oiled surface. Use a rolling pin to roll into a rectangular shape. Spread 2 cups Date Paste (recipe follows) onto flattened dough. Add a sprinkle of coconut if desired.

Roll into a long log and cut into 12 equal slices. Place swirl side up on an oiled cookie sheet with each round slightly touching each other. Allow to rise until doubled in size.

Bake at 350 degrees for 30–35 minutes.

MAKES: 12 rolls

Date Paste

2 cups **date pieces**
1 cup **water**

Boil dates and water together for 5 minutes.

Place in blender and blend until silky smooth. If needed, add more water until it is an apple butter consistency. This is wonderful in sweet rolls (instead of brown sugar and butter) or used as a sweetener in many desserts. This can also be used as a jam-like spread. Keeps refrigerated for up to two weeks.

Ezekiel 4:9 Bread

"Bread as old as the hills."

1¾ cups **warm water**, 110 to 115 degrees
1 tablespoon **+ 1 teaspoon yeast**
2 tablespoons **molasses**
½ cup **unbleached bread flour**
½ cup **soy flour**
1 cup **whole wheat flour**
½ cup **barley**
1 cup **spelt flour**
½ cup **sprouted lentils or cooked lentils**
1½ teaspoons **salt**
¼ cup **uncooked millet**

Mix well in a large bowl the warm water, yeast, and molasses until the yeast is dissolved. Let stand until foamy.

Add flours, lentils, salt, and millet to yeast mixture and mix well 3–5 minutes. Allow gluten to develop.

Add 1 cup whole wheat flour to other bread mixture in order to take away stickiness. Let the dough be slightly sticky to touch but not gooey.

Shape into a loaf and place in oiled pan Allow to rise until doubled in size.

Bake at 350 degrees for 35–40 minutes. Put bread on its side on a cooling rack for even cooling. Enjoy this ancient style bread

MAKES: 1 loaf

Spelt Bread

Preheat oven to 350 degrees.

1⅔ cups **hot water** (110–120 degrees)
¼ cup **honey**
2 teaspoons **yeast**
2 cups **spelt flour**
⅓ cup **olive oil**, optional
1½ teaspoons **salt**
3 to **4 more cups spelt flour**

Place water, honey, and yeast in a large bowl or bread mixer.

Mix together until yeast is dissolved. Let this mixture stand for 10 minutes so that your yeast can consume the sweetness of the honey and begin to let off carbon dioxide. This is what transforms your dough into an airy loaf of bread! Once you know that your yeast is active, you may add the oil, if using it, salt and spelt flour. Combine these ingredients to your yeast mixture, stirring until there are not lumps.

Add 3–4 more cups spelt flour. If you are using a bread mixer you will mix your bread dough for 2–3 minutes. If you are mixing by hand, you will mix in as much flour as you can with a spoon and then you will sprinkle the rest of your flour on your counter in a circle and flip your dough onto the flour. Now you will start pulling the edges into the middle of your dough, and keep this up for 10 minutes. The purpose of mixing the dough is to develop the gluten, which gives your dough stretchy structure. You will want your dough to be sticky to the touch but not so much as to stick to your hands too much. If it sticks to your hands, keep adding a little flour until it no longer sticks to your hands.

Place in a large oiled bowl. Allow to rise for 30–40 minutes or double in size. Shape into 2 loaves or 12 buns. Rise a second time (doubled in size) in pans.

Bake at 350 degrees for 30–35 minutes.

MAKES: 2 loaves or 12 large buns

> **Tips/Comments**
>
> Spelt versus wheat—Spelt is considered an ancient grain and the gluten in spelt is water-soluble and heat breaks it down. Some people feel better using spelt over wheat, however, it still has gluten in it and is not appropriate for those who are gluten intolerant.

Whole Wheat Buns

Preheat oven to 350 degrees.

2 cups **warm water** (110–115 degrees)
¼ cup **apple juice concentrate or honey**
2 tablespoons **yeast**
3 tablespoons **Corn Butter** (p. 59)
2½ cup **unbleached white flour**
3 cups **whole wheat flour**
1½ teaspoons **salt**

Tips/Comments

To add another dimension to this recipe, add ¾ cup finely chopped onion and 1 teaspoon dill weed.

Mix together in a large bowl water, apple juice or honey, yeast, and corn butter until yeast is dissolved. Let stand until foamy.

Add flours and salt to yeast mixture and mix well 3–5 minutes. Add up to 1 more cup whole wheat flour for proper consistency. Let the dough be slightly sticky to touch but not gooey.

Knead buns for 15 minutes to allow the gluten to develop. Shape into buns and place on a sprayed pan.

Bake at 375 degrees, for 20–25 minutes.

MAKES: 20 buns

Bread Loaf

Preheat oven to 350 degrees.

Do you like homemade whole wheat bread? You can make it from the Whole Wheat Bun recipe by making a few changes. Use less yeast, 1½ tablespoons; less or no unbleached white flour, making up the difference with whole wheat flour. Now, follow the rest of the instructions for whole wheat buns until you come to baking time and temperature. Bake at 350 degrees for 35–40 minutes. This recipe makes one 2¼ pound loaf of whole wheat bread.

Croissants

If you would like to make croissants with this recipe, use more unbleached flour and less whole wheat flour. When dough is ready to shape, roll it until it is about a ¼-inch thick, and spread with Corn Butter (p. 59). Cut the dough into triangles, roll and shape like a crescent. Allow to rise until double in size. Bake at 350 degrees for 20 minutes.

Almond Crackers

- 2 cups **almond flour**
- ½ cup **quick oats**
- ½ cup **ground flax** (I like golden best)
- ¼ teaspoon **basil**
- ½ teaspoon **salt**
- 1–3 teaspoons **nutritional yeast flakes**
- ½ teaspoon **granulated onion**
- 1 medium **tomato**
- ½ small **zucchini**
- ¼ cup **water**
- 1 tablespoon **sesame seeds**

Mix in a medium bowl almond flour, oats, ground flax, basil, salt, nutritional yeast, and granulated onion until salt is evenly distributed.

Place in a blender or bullet tomato, zucchini, water, and sesame seeds; blend well.

Mix the two sets of ingredients until the dry ingredients are moist, adding more water if needed to be able to roll out the mixture easily. Add no more than one teaspoon at a time.

Roll your mixture out like you would pie crust. I like to use two pieces of plastic wrap to roll it out between, until the mixture is as thin as pie crust. Place on a cookie sheet by taking the top plastic off and flipping onto the cookie sheet so that the plastic wrap is on top and can easily be removed.

Bake at 170 degrees for 2 hours or until mixture is completely dry. For faster baking try 250 degrees for 1½ hours. I have made these in a thin cookie shape, and it works great! Cool and store in an airtight container.

Flax Crackers

2 cups **flax seed** (golden is less pungent)
2 cups **hot water**
¼ cup **Bragg Liquid Aminos**®
Pinch of **dill weed**
Pinch of **red pepper flakes**

Place flax in a bowl and cover with hot water. Add the Bragg Liquid Aminos®, dill weed, and red pepper flakes. Stir and let set for about an hour. Flax will absorb all the liquid and becomes a gelatinous consistency.

Cover two large cookie sheets with parchment paper. Divide flax mixture in half and spread half on each cookie sheet. Spread very thinly over the parchment paper so that the mixture is basically only one flax seed deep.

Bake in a 200-degree oven for 5–6 hours. After about an hour and a half take a knife or pizza cutter, and score the crackers into desired shapes. Once they are completely dry, they will crack in odd shapes, so it's better done when they are still moist.

Store in an airtight container (if you don't eat them first!).

Whole Wheat Tortillas

3 cups **whole wheat pastry flour**
¾ teaspoon **salt**
1 teaspoon **aluminum-free baking powder, optional**
3 tablespoons **oil**
1 cup **water**

Mix flour, salt, and baking powder together in a small bowl. Emulsify water and oil together and add to the flour mixture.

> **Tips/Comments**
> For different flavors, you may add 1 tablespoon dry basil or seasoning of your choice. Sundried tomatoes blended with the water and oil adds a great flavor, too.

Knead together like bread dough, adding a little more flour if dough is a little sticky.

Divide into 12 equal portions.

Roll out in a circular shape, about the size of a pie crust, with a rolling pin. Try to get each portion thinner than a pie crust.

Place on a HOT grill, and lightly brown on each side. Place each tortilla between layers of a towel to keep moist until cool, and then store in a plastic bag.

MAKES: 12 tortillas

Savory Main Dishes

Black Bean Medley

1 medium **onion**, cut in half-rings
1 cup **carrots**, diced
1½ cups **Napa cabbage**, chopped
2 tablespoons **lemon juice**
1 teaspoon **salt**
1 teaspoon **dried garlic**
1 tablespoon **chili powder**
1 teaspoon **cayenne**
1 tablespoon **basil**
1 teaspoon **Spike**®
2 teaspoons **dill**
6 green **onions**, chopped
1 cup **spinach**, chopped
4 cups **cooked black beans,** in juice
2 cups **chopped tomatoes**

Begin by sautéing onions and carrots in a small amount of water or oil for about a minute.

Add cabbage, lemon juice, salt, spices, and herbs and sauté a few more minutes.

Add green onions and continue to sauté. I like to use green tops down to the white just above the roots. (I have planted roots in potting soil, and they grow!)

Stir in black beans, tomatoes, and spinach. Stir until all are well heated.

Serve over brown rice, quinoa or pasta topped with a dollop of Tofutti® Sour Cream and chopped fresh cilantro. This is SO good it's sure to become a favorite!

SERVES: 8

Stroganoff

1 pound **firm tofu**, cut into cubes
3 tablespoons **Chicken-style Seasoning** (p. 64)
3 tablespoons **tamari**
2 tablespoons **water (& oil if desired)**
Use one recipe of **Cashew Gravy (5 cups)** (p. 61)
1½ cups **chopped broccoli**
1 cup **carrot circles**
1½ cups **chopped cauliflower**
1 **onion** sliced into half moons

Mix Chicken-style Seasoning, tamari, and water (& oil, if desired) together well.

Pour over cubed tofu and allow to marinate for 10 minutes.

Place in a single layer on a sprayed baking pan and bake for ½ hour at 350 degrees or until slightly crispy.

Sauté vegetables in a small amount of water or oil until al dente. Add Cashew Gravy.

Serve this over pasta (or rice), enjoy a great "Veggie" Stroganoff meal.

SERVES: 8

Spring Rolls

1 package **mung bean threads**
3 green **onions, tops & all, chopped**
1¼ cups **shredded carrots**
1 (10-ounce) **package frozen snow peas**
1 package **fresh bean sprouts**
⅓ pound **fresh spinach**
1 tablespoon **fresh ginger**
2 tablespoons **cilantro, chopped**
⅓ cup **tamari soy sauce**
1 teaspoon **cornstarch**
1 pound **Baked Tofu** (p. 41)
1 package **rice wraps**

Soak mung bean threads in HOT water for 5 minutes. Chop into 3-inch strips.

Sauté green onions, carrots, snow peas, spinach, bean sprouts, chopped ginger and cilantro in a small amount of oil or water.

Mix tamari and cornstarch together for a minute.

Add rice noodles, tofu cubes and tamari mixture to sautéed vegetables. Heat a few minutes, mixing all the while.

Using a large scoop, place a scoop of mixture in the middle of a soaked rice wrap. Fold and roll; place seam side down on a sprayed baking sheet. Repeat. When the pan is full, spray each spring roll with a small amount of pan spray.

Bake at 350 degrees for 10–15 minutes. Serve with warm Sweet Chile Sauce (p. 66) over the top.

MAKES: 24

Basic Oat Burgers

¼ cup **nutritional yeast flakes**
⅔ cup **soy sauce**
¼ cup **sunflower seeds**
1 tablespoon **garlic powder**
1 tablespoon **basil**

2 teaspoons **onion powder**
1 teaspoon **coriander**
¾ cup **walnuts**
1 teaspoon **sage**
4 cups **old-fashioned rolled oats**

Place yeast flakes, soy sauce, sunflower seeds, garlic powder, basil, onion powder, coriander, walnuts, and sage in a large pan with 4 cups of water, and bring to a boil over medium heat.

Stir in oats. Mix together and let simmer for one minute.

Set aside until cooled, then form into burgers and place on a sprayed cookie sheet.

Bake at 350 degrees for 15 minutes on each side.

MAKES: 12 burgers

> **Tips/Comments**
>
> After you have baked these, you can enjoy them fresh from the oven or freeze them for use later. Also, when burgers are cool, crumble them into small pieces, and use as you would ground beef.

Chickpea Burgers

2 cups **chickpeas (garbanzo beans)**
1 cup **hot water**
¼ cup **Chicken-style Seasoning** (p. 64)
¼ cup **soy sauce**
1 cup **walnuts**
2 teaspoons **sage**
1 large **onion**, chopped
4 cups **old-fashioned oats**

Blend chickpeas, water, seasoning, soy sauce, walnuts, sage, and onion together in food processor or blender until smooth.

Add the oats and let stand for 15 minutes.

Form into burgers and place on a sprayed cookie sheet.

Bake at 350 for 15 minutes, turn and bake for 5–10 minutes longer.

Serve with favorite toppings.

YIELD: 12 burgers

Bean Burgers

4 cups **water**
4 cups **bean soup***
½ cup **soy sauce**
¾ cup **shredded carrots**
¾ cup **salsa**
¼ cup **nutritional yeast flakes**
1 tablespoon **basil**
½ tablespoon **sage**
1 tablespoon **onion powder**
½ teaspoon **red chili pepper flakes**
4 cups **oats (half thick oats & half quick oats)**
½ cup **sunflower seeds**, optional
1 cup **walnuts**, optional

Place water, bean soup, soy sauce, carrots, salsa, and seasonings in a stockpot and bring to a boil.

Stir in oats, seeds, and nuts, return to a simmer for one minute.

Set aside to cool. When cooled, place a large scoop on a sprayed baking pan and pat down into a large burger. Repeat until all the mixture is panned.

Bake at 350 degrees for 30 minutes on the first side, flip, and bake for

Tips/Comments
This is a good place to use your leftovers. I dump everything in the blender with a couple of cups of beans and pulse a few times to get rid of large pieces, or you can just use refried beans instead.

an additional 15 minutes. If you like them real moist, bake for 15 minutes on each side. These freeze really well after they are baked. They can be reheated on the BBQ grill if you like.

MAKES: 18 large burgers

By using Scrambled Tofu (Pg. 15), adding Vegenaise®, diced onion, pickle and celery, you can make a "chicken salad" sandwich. Top it off with lettuce, tomato, sprouts and onion cut in rings.

Falafel

3 cups **water**
1 cup **oats**
½ cup **millet**
4 cups **bread crumbs**
½ cup **walnuts**
½ cup **sunflower seeds**
1¼ cups **of cooked garbanzo beans**
½ cup **dried parsley**

¼ cup **honey**
3 tablespoons **granulated onion**
3 tablespoons **tahini**
1 tablespoon **granulated garlic**
2 teaspoons **cumin**
½ teaspoon **coriander**
½ teaspoon **Spike®**

Bring water to a boil and add the oats and millet. Simmer for 30 minutes to completely cook the millet.

Place bread, walnuts, and sunflower seeds in a food processor with the "S" blade and process until nuts are very fine. Add garbanzo beans to food processor and process. Add oats and millet along with parsley, onion, cumin, coriander, Spike®, honey, and tahini. Process everything together to make a sticky mixture.

Scoop out to the desired size onto sprayed cookie sheet, either for round Falafel balls or make these into burger shapes for Falafel burgers.

Bake at 350 degrees, 25 minutes for falafel balls or 15 minutes on each side for burgers. This makes a large batch. Use them fresh and freeze the rest for future use.

MAKES: 40 Falafel balls or 18 burgers

Mexican Lasagna

3 cups **cooked black beans**, rinsed
3 cups **diced tomatoes**
¾ cup **chopped green chilies**
3 cups **corn** (frozen okay)
6 chopped **green onions**
1½ tablespoons **dried oregano**
1 tablespoon **chili seasoning**
1½ tablespoons **cumin**
2 cups **Melty Cheese** (p. 57)
8 corn **tortillas**, cut into slices

Combine beans, tomatoes, chilies, corn, green onions, cumin, oregano, and chili seasoning in a large skillet; heat thoroughly.

Spray a large baking dish. Line this baking dish with 1/2 of the tortillas, overlapping tortillas if necessary.

Spread half of bean-vegetable mixture over tortillas.

Spread with half of Melty Cheese. Repeat.

Bake at 350 degrees for 35 minutes.

SERVES: 6–8

Lasagna

1 pound **firm tofu**
½ teaspoon **salt,**
½ teaspoon **garlic powder**
1 teaspoon **onion powder**
9 lasagna **noodles**
1 large **onion,** chopped
3 cloves **garlic, minced**
½ cup **green pepper**, chopped
4 cups **crushed tomatoes**
2 teaspoons **apple juice concentrate**
1 tablespoon **Italian seasoning**
1 teaspoon **sweet basil**
½ teaspoon **oregano**
1 teaspoon **salt**
1 teaspoon **paprika**
Cashew Jack Cheese (recipe follows)

Crumble tofu in a bowl. Sprinkle with the salt, garlic powder, and onion powder. Set aside to meld.

Cook and drain nine lasagna noodles.

Sauté onion, garlic, and peppers in small amount of water (or oil). Add tomatoes, juice concentrate, Italian seasoning, basil, oregano, salt, paprika, and cheese, and simmer for 10 minutes to blend flavors.

Cashew Jack Cheese

1 cup **cashews**
½ cup **chopped onions**
¼ teaspoon **garlic powder**
2 tablespoons **lemon juice**
1 tablespoon **nutritional yeast flakes**
¾ teaspoon **salt**

Blend in a blender cashews, onions, garlic powder, lemon juice, nutritional yeast flakes, and salt with 1 cup hot water. Place one cup of water in a small saucepan over medium heat, add mixture from blender and stir constantly for a couple of minutes, or until thickened.

To Assemble Lasagna: Cover bottom of baking dish with a thin layer of sauce. Make alternate layers of noodles, tofu, cheese sauce, and tomato sauce. Cover top with tomato sauce and garnish with Cashew Jack Cheese.

SERVES: 12

Italian Sauce

1 medium **onion**, diced
1 tablespoon **basil**
1 tablespoon **Pizza Seasoning (Italian)**
1 tablespoon **onion powder**
½ tablespoon **garlic powder**
½ teaspoon **oregano**
½ teaspoon **savory**
½ to 1 teaspoon **red chili peppers**
6 cups **tomato sauce**

Sauté onion in small amount of water or oil.

Add seasonings to onions and sauté for a few seconds to bring out flavors. Add tomato sauce, and bring to a simmer.

Simmer for 5 minutes.

Potato Patties

6 cooked **potatoes** (these could be leftovers)
1 teaspoon **onion powder**
1 cup **nut or soy milk**
1–2 tablespoons **dried or fresh parsley**
Vege-Sal® seasoning **salt** to taste (¼ teaspoon)

Mix into the potatoes while still hot onion powder, milk, parsley, and Vege-Sal® to make a mashed potato type mixture.

Add raw shredded potato, and mix in well. This mixture should be moist.

Form into patties and place on a sprayed cookie sheet.

Bake at 400 degrees for 15 minutes and turn. Bake an additional 15 minutes or until golden brown.

MAKES: 12 (½-cup) patties

Tasty "Cheese" Enchiladas

Cashew Cheese mixture:

¾ cup **raw cashews**
¼ cup **raw sunflower seeds**
1 tablespoon **onion powder**
2 teaspoons **garlic powder**
1 tablespoon **lemon juice**
1 cup **warm water**

Tofu mixture:

20 ounces **tofu**, crumbled
½ teaspoon **salt**
2 tablespoons **fresh parsley**
½ cup **diced green chilies**

Blend cashews, sunflower seeds, onion powder, garlic powder, lemon juice, and water together in a blender until very smooth.

Mix tofu, salt, parsley, and green chilies together along with cashew mixture and set aside.

Sauce:

2 cups **tomato sauce**
½ teaspoon **chili powder**
½ teaspoon **oregano**
¼ teaspoon **cumin**
1 tablespoon **flour** (optional)
⅔ cup **water**

Assembly Directions:

12 (6-inch) **tortillas (corn or wheat)**
1 cup **cooked beans** (if desired)

Dip tortillas, one at a time, in sauce and fill each one with about ¼ cup of tofu mixture (if using beans add a tablespoon at this time).

Roll and place uniformly in sprayed casserole dish, fold down. If desired, you may put a tablespoon of Cashew Cheese mixture in each enchilada.

Top with extra sauce.

Bake at 350 degrees for 30 minutes. May top with grated slicing cheese or put Cashew Cheese mixture in a squirt bottle and squirt on the top.

Suggestions: Garnish with a side of shredded Romaine lettuce, diced fresh tomatoes, a bit of salsa and guacamole for a colorful meal!

MAKES: 18

> **Tips/Comments**
>
> I let the mouse run away with the dairy cheese for this recipe. "Depending on the type, cheese is 20 to 50% milkfat. Of that, about 40% is saturated! Cheese is high in calories and sodium" (Roehl, Evelyn, *Whole Foods Facts*, p. 3).

Quinoa Risotto

2 cups **quinoa**
2 tablespoons **Chicken-style Seasoning (p.** 64)
2 cups **carrots, julienne**
1 garlic **clove**, crushed
1 red **onion**, cut into half-moons
1 red **pepper**, cut into strips
¼ pound of **spinach**

Mix 3½ cups water and Chicken-style Seasoning together and bring to a boil. Add the quinoa and simmer about 20 minutes.

Sauté carrots, garlic, onion, pepper, and spinach in a small amount of water or oil until al dente.

Place cooked vegetables over cooked quinoa. Sprinkle with Walnut Parmesan Cheese (p. 65) and serve.

SERVES: 8

Volcanoes

44 blue **corn chips (11 chips in a serving)**
2 cups **beans**, your choice
2 cups **cooked rice**
4 cups **shredded lettuce**
½ cup **salsa**
½ cup **guacamole**
½ cup **sour cream**
½ cup **chopped green onion**
½ cup **chopped tomatoes**
½ cup or 1 can **sliced black olives (2.25 ounces)**

(This recipe serves four by dividing the above ingredients into fourths).

Start your volcano with a serving of chips.

Top with beans, rice, lettuce, salsa, guacamole, sour cream, green onions, tomatoes, and black olives. Hopefully, it will not explode all over your plate!

SERVES: 4

Tamale Pie

1 cup **chopped onion**
1 green **pepper**, chopped
1 teaspoon **cumin**
½ teaspoon **oregano**
⅛ teaspoon **cayenne**
1 cup **sliced black olives**
½ teaspoon **garlic powder**
½ cup **fresh cilantro**
1 cup **frozen corn**
2 cups **chopped tomatoes**
1 teaspoon **salt**
1–1½ cups **nut or soy milk**
1 cup **cornmeal**

Sauté onion and green pepper in small amount of water. Add cumin, oregano, cayenne, olives, garlic powder, cilantro, corn, tomatoes, and salt.

Mix the cold milk and cornmeal together and add to vegetable mixture.

Cook over medium heat until mixture is thickened, stirring constantly.

Pour into a sprayed medium-sized baking dish (for a different flair, cook in a cast iron skillet or pour into a cupcake tin to make individual servings).

Bake at 350 degrees for 1 hour. Best reheated and served the next day.

*Top with a dollop of Melty Cheese (p. 57).

SERVES: 8

> **Tips/Comments**
> You may add spinach leaves for more color and leftover beans may be added for more protein.

Mazidra

8 cups **water**
4 cups **green lentils**
1 tablespoon **marjoram**
1 teaspoon **thyme**
3 tablespoons **Chicken-style Seasoning** (p. 64)
2 bay **leaves**
2 cups **chopped onions**
1 cup **diced tomatoes**
¼ cup **soy sauce**
1 cup **tomato puree**

Bring water to a boil in a large stockpot and place lentils in the boiling water. Cover and cook on low heat.

After 20–30 minutes when lentils are al dente, add marjoram, thyme, Chicken-style Seasoning, bay leaves, onions, tomatoes, soy sauce, and tomato puree. Cook another 10–15 minutes.

Serve over brown rice. Top with lettuce, salsa, guacamole, and olives, and surround with baked corn chips.

SERVES: 12

Peanut Butter Pasta

12 ounces **linguine noodles**, cooked and drained
Peanut Butter Sauce (recipe follows)
½ cup **chopped green onion**
½ cup **whole peanuts**

Peanut Butter Sauce

⅔ cup **peanut butter**
2 tablespoons **soy sauce**
⅓ cup **lemon juice**
4 garlic **cloves, pressed**
2 pinches **cayenne**
1½ cups **water**

> **Tips/Comments**
> Did you know? "Peanuts are legumes, like beans and peas. But the pods grow underground, much like potatoes" (Roehl, Evelyn, *Whole Foods Facts* by Evelyn Roehl, p. 104).

Blend peanut butter, soy sauce, lemon juice, garlic, cayenne, and water until smooth to make Peanut Butter Sauce.

Place in a small saucepan and bring to a boil.

Toss with cooked linguine and top with chopped green onions and whole peanuts.

SERVES: 8

Hunan

1 cup **chopped broccoli**
½ cup **chopped red pepper**
1 (10–12 ounce) package water-packed **tofu**
Peanut Butter Sauce (p. 39)

Sauté vegetables, leaving them crunchy but well heated.

Add crumbled tofu to Peanut Butter Sauce, along with sautéed vegetables and serve over a bed of short grain brown rice.

SERVES: 4 to 6

Sautéed Mushrooms

24 ounces **fresh mushrooms**
½ cup **Corn Butter** (p. 59)

Wash and slice mushrooms. Melt corn butter and sauté sliced mushrooms. Delightful!

The Fajita Meal

Baked Tofu

1 pound **of tofu strips**
1 tablespoon **tahini**
2 tablespoons **soy sauce**
2 tablespoons **hot water**
1 tablespoon **Chicken-style Seasoning**
(p. 64)

Marinate the tofu strips in the tahini, soy sauce, hot water, and Chicken-style Seasoning. Place on parchment paper or a sprayed cookie sheet.

Bake in a hot oven, about 400 degrees, until crispy and browned.

Veggies for Fajitas

1 red **pepper**, sliced
1 medium size **yellow onion**, sliced
1 green **pepper**, sliced
1 yellow **pepper**, sliced
3 medium size **tomatoes** cut into eighths
1½ tablespoons **chili powder**
1 cup **mushrooms**, sliced
Spinach leaves (optional)

Sauté peppers, onion, and mushrooms for a few minutes on medium heat. Add tomatoes for the last few minutes.

To assemble: Place spinach leaves on a tortilla, top with veggies and baked tofu. Garnish with guacamole and salsa.

Whole wheat tortillas can be found in your local grocery or health food store, often found in the frozen food section. I like to use whole wheat in this meal and whenever possible.

SERVES: 6

> **Tips/Comments**
> Peppers. What are they? "Mild to hot … green, red, yellow. Peppers are fruits of a plant that is related to tomatoes and eggplant, part of the nightshade family" (Roehl, Evelyn, *Whole Foods Facts*, p. 145).

Stir Fry

6 cups **assorted fresh vegetables** (carrots, onions, broccoli, celery, peppers, pea pods, water chestnuts, etc.)

Sauté the vegetables in a small amount of water in a nonstick skillet or wok, until just slightly cooked but still crispy. To this mixture, you may add some frozen peas, fresh spinach, or pineapple chunks, and a few toasted nuts, if desired. Your YIELD will vary depending on the amount of vegetables used.

Add Oriental Sauce (p. 42) and serve over Dextrinized Brown Rice (p. 43).

SERVES: 4 to 6

Summer Vegetable Casserole

1 small **onion** cut into rings
1 cup **celery**, chopped
2 cups **summer squash**, thinly sliced
2 cups **zucchini squash**, thinly sliced
1 tablespoon **Italian seasoning**
1 (15-ounce) can **diced tomatoes**, about 1½ cups

Sauté the onion, celery, summer squash, and zucchini in a small amount of water or cooking oil.

Add tomatoes and Italian seasoning when tender. Simmer to meld flavors.

Serve over a bed of rice or Quinoa topped with toasted sunflower seeds.

SERVES: 6

Oriental Sauce

½ cup **soy sauce**
1½ tablespoons **lemon juice**
1½ cup **cold water**
1 tablespoon **apple juice concentrate**
2–3 tablespoons **cornstarch**
1 tablespoon **tahini**

Emulsify tahini in cold water along with soy sauce, lemon juice, water, juice concentrate, and cornstarch until tahini is well dissolved.

Thicken over medium heat, stirring constantly.

MAKES: 2 cups

Dextrinized Brown Rice

Toast 2 cups of brown rice, lightly, in a large skillet by placing the rice in the skillet that is on medium heat. Stir the rice constantly so that it will not become too dark. Add 4 cups of water and bring to a boil. Turn heat to low and simmer for 1 hour. Do not remove lid during cooking time as moisture will be lost and rice will not cook as thoroughly.

MAKES: 4 (1-cup) servings

Baked Tofu 2

Marinate 1 pound of **tofu chunks** in the following:
¼ cup **soy sauce**
Or
¼ cup **Oriental Sauce**

Place on a cookie sheet.

Bake in a hot oven, about 400 degrees, until crispy and browned, turning once.

SERVES: 4

The Stroganoff Meal

Brazil Nut Gravy

1 cup **Brazil nuts***
3 tablespoons **soy sauce**
1½ tablespoons **onion powder**
¼ cup **cornstarch**
1 tablespoon **Chicken-style Seasoning** (p. 64)
½ teaspoon **salt**
2 tablespoons **nutritional yeast flakes**
4 cups **water**

Blend nuts, soy sauce, onion powder, cornstarch, Chicken-style Seasoning, salt, and nutritional yeast flakes thoroughly in a blender, adding water slowly.

> **Tips/Comments**
> You will thoroughly enjoy Brazil Nut Gravy! It's great with mashed potatoes, over biscuits and in any way you would use gravy.
>
> You may substitute cashews for Brazil nuts.

Simmer mixture until thickened, adding more water if necessary.

MAKES 10 (½-cup) servings

Veggies and Noodles

2 pounds of **veggies,** such as **a mixture of fresh or frozen broccoli, cauliflower, and carrots.**
2 large **red or yellow onions** cut in rings
1–1¼ pounds **of fettuccine noodles**, cooked and drained

Sauté chopped or sliced vegetables and onions.

Place cooked pasta in a pasta dish.

Spread sautéed vegetables over the top and cover with Brazil Nut Gravy (p. 43)

SERVES: 6 to 8

Pasta with White Beans

2 tablespoons **extra-virgin olive oil**
1 teaspoon **minced garlic**
2–3 cups **rinsed white kidney beans**
4 cups **diced fresh tomatoes**
½ cup **fresh torn basil**, lightly packed
1 teaspoon **salt** or to taste
½ pound **shell pasta**

Sauté garlic in olive oil or a small amount of water.

Add the beans, tomatoes, basil, and salt.

Cook your pasta by following the package directions. Drain while reserving ⅓ cup of cooking water.

Toss together with the veggie mixture and the reserved cooking water. Enjoy!

SERVES: 4

Pasta with Collard Greens

1 pound **cooked shell pasta**
1 tablespoon **extra-virgin olive oil** or
2 tablespoons **water**
3½ cups **diced Roma tomatoes**
¼ cup **chopped fresh basil**
1 teaspoon **minced garlic**
½ teaspoon **salt**
3–4 cups **chopped collard greens or greens of your choice**

Sauté tomatoes, basil, garlic, salt, and greens in oil or water for 2–3 minutes in a large skillet. Add the cooked pasta to the skillet and toss all ingredients together until well heated. Serve right away.

SERVES: 6

Tips/Comments
This is a tasty way to use summer greens.

Succotash
(Fall Medley)

1½ pounds **butternut squash**
1 cup **chopped onion**
1 medium **red pepper**, diced
4 ounces **green chilies**
2 teaspoons **finely minced garlic**
¾ teaspoon **cumin**

2 tablespoons **tomato paste**
1 tablespoon **Spike®**
¼ cup **minced fresh cilantro**
2 cups **frozen baby lima beans**
2 cups **fresh or frozen corn**

Peel and dice squash into small cubes, a little smaller than an inch square.

Sauté the diced squash, onion, pepper, green chilies, and garlic in a small amount of water or olive oil until slightly browned.

Add 1 cup water, cumin, tomato paste, Spike®, and cilantro. Simmer till squash is tender. Add corn and lima beans.

Cook until all ingredients come to a slight boil.

This can be served alone or on a bed of brown rice or quinoa.

SERVES: 8

Wild Rice Casserole

2 cups of **wild rice**
1 medium **red onion**, chopped
1 red **pepper**, diced
1 green **pepper**, diced
6 cups **diced tomatoes**

2 cups **sliced olives**
⅓ cup **Chicken-style Seasoning** (p. 64)
½ cup **flax seed**, ground fine

Bring the 5 cups of water to a boil and add the wild rice; cook together for approximately one hour. The rice should curl and show it's white inside.

Sauté the onions and peppers for a few minutes in a small amount of water or olive oil.

Add to the sautéed peppers the cooked rice

along with tomatoes, olives, and Chicken-style Seasoning. Mix together well. Add the ground flax seed. Mix all ingredients together until well blended. You may bake as a casserole dish or scoop into balls.

Bake at 350 degrees for 15 minutes. Serve with a scoop of Cashew Gravy (p. 61) drizzled over the top.

SERVES: 12

Harvest Nut Roast

2 cups **chopped onions**
1½ cups **soy milk**
3 cups **finely chopped celery**
⅔ cup **chopped walnuts**
⅔ cup **chopped pecans**
½ cup **sunflower seeds**
1 tablespoon **basil**
1½ teaspoons **sage**
1½ teaspoons **salt**
4–5 cups **soft whole wheat bread crumbs**

Sauté the onions in small amount of water or oil (olive), along with the celery. Sometimes I use broccoli stems instead of celery. It's a good substitute for those who don't like celery and a good way to use up broccoli stems.

Place the walnuts, pecans, sunflower seeds, basil, sage and salt into a large bowl. Add the onions and celery. Mix together. Fold in bread crumbs.

Place all ingredients in a sprayed baking dish or make into ½ cup mounds.

Bake at 350 degrees for 1 hour if it's a loaf pan or ½ hour for mounds. To prevent over browning on top, may need to cover with foil near the end of baking.

SERVES: 8

Pecan Tofu Balls

½ cup **toasted pecans**, finely chopped
1 cup **whole wheat soft bread**, cut in cubes
½ pound **tofu**, crumbled
1 tablespoon **whole wheat flour**
2 tablespoons **flax seed**, ground fine
½ small **red onion, minced**
2 tablespoons **nutritional yeast flakes**
1 tablespoon **fresh parsley**, chopped
½ teaspoon **salt**
½ teaspoon **sage**
½ teaspoon **marjoram**
2 tablespoons **sesame seeds**
1 tablespoon **Bragg Liquid Aminos**®
¼ teaspoon **each onion and garlic powder**
½ teaspoon **Pizza Seasoning** (p. 122)

Place pecans in a single layer on a baking sheet and toast at 350 degrees for 8–10 minutes. Be sure to watch them, so they don't overcook. Chop after toasting.

Combine toasted pecans, cut up bread, and crumbled tofu in a large bowl. Sprinkle with whole wheat flour, ground flax, minced onion, nutritional yeast flakes, parsley, salt, sage, marjoram, sesame seeds, Bragg Liquid Aminos®, onion powder, garlic powder, and Pizza Seasoning. Mix together well.

Form into balls and place on a sprayed cookie sheet.

Bake at 350 degrees for 15 minutes.

MAKES: 12 balls

Ensenada Casserole

1¼ cups **long grain brown rice**
½ tablespoon **onion powder**
½ tablespoon **chili powder**
1 teaspoon **garlic powder**
1 teaspoon **cumin**
½ teaspoon **salt**
2 cups **broccoli**, chopped
1 small **onion**, chopped
1 red **pepper**, chopped
1 green **pepper**, chopped
½ cup **green chilies**, chopped
2 cups **kernel corn**, frozen
1 tablespoon **cumin**
4 cups **refried beans**; canned is good

Bring 3 cups water to a boil; place onion powder, chili powder garlic powder, cumin, and salt along with the rice into the boiling water. Cover and reduce heat to low and cook for 45 minutes and set aside.

Prepare a batch of Melty Cheese (p. 57) and set aside.

Sauté broccoli, onion, peppers, chilies, corn, and cumin in a small amount of water or oil. Leave them slightly crispy.

Coat an 8x13-inch pan with cooking spray. Spread all the rice on the bottom, next, as evenly as you can spread the refried beans. Sprinkle veggies over beans and top with Melty Cheese.

Tips/Comments: Ensenada also makes great burritos. Once you have enjoyed the casserole, take your leftovers and place ¾ to 1 cup in a tortilla shell and wrap into a burrito. Burritos can be frozen for future use by wrapping them in foil.

Bake at 350 degrees for 30 minutes. When serving, top with salsa (p. 54) and garnish with corn chips.

SERVES: 12

Ratatouille

1 **eggplant**, cut into cubes
2 small **zucchinis**, sliced
1 small **onion**, chopped
2 garlic **cloves**, crushed
2 red **peppers**, chopped
2 green **peppers**, chopped
1 teaspoon **thyme**
1 teaspoon **basil**
½ tablespoon **rosemary**
½ teaspoon **coriander**
½ teaspoon **salt**
3 cups **diced tomatoes**

Toss eggplant and zucchini in small amount of olive oil. Spread on a sprayed baking pan. Roast in 350-degree oven, until lightly browned (about 20–30 minutes).

Sauté onions, garlic, and peppers in small amount of water or olive oil. Add thyme, basil, rosemary, coriander, and salt, and sauté a little longer.

Add tomatoes and the roasted eggplant and zucchini. Heat completely.

Serve over couscous, rice or quinoa.

SERVES: 12

Tasty Cereal Loaf

1 large **onion**, finely chopped
2 (12-ounce) **packages silken tofu**
⅓ cup **Chicken-style Seasoning** (p. 64)
½ cup **chopped nuts**
6–7 cups **Special K®** or similar cereal

Sauté onion in ¼ cup of water, or Corn Butter (p. 59) or a vegan margarine.

Crumble tofu in a large bowl; add Chicken-style Seasoning and let marinate together for a few minutes. Add nuts and Special-K® or similar cereal—do not crush. Next, add the sautéed onions and mix together.

Place in sprayed 9x13-inch baking dish.

Bake at 350 degrees for 45 minutes.

SERVES: 12

Chickpea A La King

1 cup **chopped yellow onion**
1½ cups **chopped red pepper**
2 cups **sliced mushrooms** (optional)
1 cup **chopped celery**
3 cups **cooked chickpeas**
3 cups **green peas, frozen or fresh**
2 cups **raw cashews**
1½ tablespoons **cornstarch**

2 tablespoons **sesame seeds**
5 tablespoons **Country-style Seasoning** (p. 64)
¼ cup **soy sauce (Bragg Liquid Aminos®)**
2 teaspoons **garlic powder**
1½ tablespoons **onion powder**
1½ cups **hot water** (last)

Sauté the onions, peppers, mushrooms and celery in a small amount of water, then add the chickpeas and green peas. Heat until peas are al dente and set aside for later.

Blend cashews, cornstarch, sesame seeds, Country-style Seasoning, soy sauce, garlic powder, and onion powder on high until smooth, adding water slowly for a creamy cashew mixture.

Bring an additional 3 cups of water to a boil in a medium saucepan, add the cashew mixture slowly and thicken as you would gravy. Stir while this is coming to a boil to keep from sticking. Place sautéed vegetables over a bed of fettuccini pasta, brown rice, or quinoa and top with cashew sauce.

SERVES: 8–10

Tips/Comments
For "Asparagus A La King" add 3 cups of chopped asparagus.

Wild Rice Stir Fry

1 cup **wild rice**
1 tablespoon **Chicken-style Seasoning** (p. 64)
1 red **bell pepper**, cut into strips
1 green **bell pepper**, cut into strips
1 medium **carrot**, cut in diagonals
1 red **onion**, cut into half-moons
2 cups **broccoli florets**, optional
½ cup **Earth Balance® Margarine**

Bring 2½ cups of water to a boil, add wild rice. Turn down to a low simmer and allow to cook for 1 hour, covered. When cooked add Chicken-style Seasoning.

Sauté cut peppers, carrots, onions and broccoli in Earth Balance® Margarine.

Serve over cooked wild rice. If you desire, you can add a little Chicken-style Seasoning to the veggies.

SERVES: 6

Tofu Yung Patties

½ cup **chopped onion**
½ cup **chopped celery**
½ cup **chopped red pepper**
1 small **potato** (¾ **cup**), shredded
½ pound **of tofu** (**8 ounces**), mashed
1 cup **cooked brown rice**
½ cup **whole wheat flour or gluten-free flour** mixed with 1 tablespoon ground flax seed
2 tablespoons **soy sauce**
3 tablespoons **nutritional yeast flakes**
1 teaspoon **onion powder**
½ teaspoon **garlic powder**
½ cup **sesame seeds**

Sauté onion, celery, red pepper, and potato in a small amount of water or oil.

Add tofu, rice, flour, soy sauce, nutritional yeast flakes, onion powder, garlic powder, and sesame seeds to a medium mixing bowl. Mix together until well blended.

Form into patties.

Bake on sprayed cookie sheet at 350 degrees for 15 minutes on each side.

MAKES: 8 patties

> **Tips/Comments**
> As an addition to these patties, you can add fresh bean sprouts to your mixture before baking.

Gluten Steaks

2 cups **gluten flour or vital wheat gluten**
1 teaspoon **basil**
2 tablespoons **unbleached all-purpose flour**
2 tablespoons **Chicken-style Seasoning** (p. 64)
1 tablespoon **onion powder**
1 teaspoon **Vege-Sal**®
1 tablespoon **garlic powder**
1½ cups **water**

Place gluten flour, basil, flour, Chicken-style seasoning, onion powder, Vege-Sal®, and garlic powder in a large bowl. Stir herbs and flour with a large spoon until well mixed.

Add water all at once, stir quickly, and then knead by hand, forming a stiff loaf. Flatten to about 1/2-inch thickness. Let it rest while preparing the Savory Broth recipe that follows.

Cut two-inch pieces or cut into strips off of the gluten loaf once the broth is ready. Drop strips or pieces into boiling broth.

Boil for 30 minutes.

Gluten steaks can be added to Harvest Nut Roast (p. 46) or breaded, fried and served with Cashew Gravy (p. 61).

MAKES: 8 gluten steaks

Savory Broth

8 cups **water**
1 teaspoon **thyme**
½ cup **soy sauce**
½ teaspoon **cumin**
1 tablespoon **onion powder**
½ teaspoon **cardamom**
1 tablespoon **garlic powder**

Place water, thyme, soy sauce, cumin, onion powder, cardamom, and garlic powder in a large saucepan. Mix together well.

Bring to a low boil. Drop in gluten pieces, simmering for 30 minutes. Remove gluten pieces with a slotted spoon. Remaining broth can be thickened and used as gravy.

MAKES: 8 cups

Green Enchiladas

Sauce

½ cup **cashews**
1 cup **green chilies**
¾ cup **sunflower seeds**
½ cup **Chicken-style Seasoning** (p. 64)
¾ cup **oats**
2 teaspoons **onion powder**
1½ teaspoons **cumin**
½ cup **lemon juice**
1 cup **spinach leaves,** for color

Blend cashews, chilies, sunflower seeds, Chicken-style Seasoning, oats, onion powder, cumin, lemon juice, and spinach until very smooth, about 2 minutes. While blending, place 4 cups of water in a saucepan and bring to a boil.

Add blended ingredients to boiling water, rinse blender with one more cup of water, add to boiling mixture and stir until it bubbles. This is the sauce for the top of the enchiladas.

Filling

1 cup **chopped black olives**
3 cups **refried beans**, your choice
½ cup **chopped red onion**
1½ cups **Green Enchilada Sauce** (above)
24 **corn tortillas**

Mix together olives, onions, beans, and Green Enchilada Sauce.

Roll this mixture in a corn tortilla, about ¼ cup at a time.

Place in a sprayed pan and pour the remaining Green Enchilada Sauce over the top.

Bake at 350 degrees for 30 minutes. Serve Hot!

MAKES: 24

Quinoa Loaf

1 cup **quinoa**
1½ cups **water**
¼ cup **Tahini (sesame butter)**
¼ cup **soy sauce**
1 cup **grated carrots**
1 cup **chopped spinach**
½ cup **chopped onion**
½ cup **chopped cashews**, optional
1½ teaspoons **garlic powder**
1½ teaspoons **thyme**
1½ teaspoons **sage**
½ teaspoon **salt**

Bring water to a boil and stir in quinoa. Simmer covered about 20 minutes. When quinoa is tender, add Tahini to hot quinoa.

Place quinoa-tahini mixture in a large bowl. Add soy sauce, carrots, spinach, onion, cashews, garlic powder, thyme, sage, and salt to the bowl with the quinoa and mix well.

Place in a sprayed baking dish and cover.

Bake at 350 degrees for 1 hour.

I like to use a large ice cream scoop (about 1/4 cup) to make mounds for quinoa balls or shape into patties. Bake for 30 minutes, turning patties once. Uncover the last 10 minutes. Serve with Cashew Gravy (p. 61).

SERVES: 8

> **Tips/Comments**
> If you are having a hard time getting the mixture to stick together as well as you like, try this. Blend 1 tablespoon flax meal, 1/2 cup hot water, and 1 tablespoon olive oil in a blender to make an egg yolk type mixture. Now mix this with the Quinoa Loaf to help it stick together better.

Spreads, Gravies & Miscellaneous

Hummus

1 (15-ounce) can **garbanzo beans**
½ cup **tahini**
1 tablespoon **olive oil**, optional
2 garlic **cloves**
2 tablespoons **lemon juice**

Heat garbanzo beans with a small amount of their liquid. They are easier to blend when they are warm and make a paste much faster.

Place the garbanzo beans, tahini, oil, garlic, and lemon juice in a blender or food processor. Process until pudding-like mixture, adding additional liquid if needed.

MAKES: 2 cups

> **Tips/Comments**
>
> Hummus traditionally is made with garbanzo beans and olive oil. Both can be optional. You can use whatever kind of bean you desire, edamame, white kidney, or even black-eyed peas. Tahini, in my opinion, is a key ingredient for hummus—without it hummus is not as creamy.

Salsa

4 cups **diced tomatoes**
2 tablespoons **chili powder**
¾ cup **minced onion**
1½ teaspoons **dried cilantro**
¾ cup **minced green pepper**
½ cup **green chilies**
½ teaspoon **dried garlic**
1 teaspoon **salt**
1 teaspoon **dried chili peppers**

Mix tomatoes, chili powder, onion, cilantro, green pepper, green chilies, garlic, salt, and dried chili peppers together.

Chill and serve. If needed, add a tablespoon or two of water to desired consistency.

MAKES: 6 cups

Creamy Herb Schmear

2 cups **warm water**
1 teaspoon **agar-agar powder**
1½ cups **cashews, raw**
3 tablespoons **lemon juice**
2 tablespoons **nutritional yeast flakes**
1 tablespoon **basil**, optional
1½ teaspoons **salt**
1 teaspoon **onion powder**
1 teaspoon **garlic powder**
1 teaspoon **dill weed**, optional
1 teaspoon **parsley**, optional
1 teaspoon **Chicken-style Seasoning** (p. 64)
1 teaspoon **dried chives**, optional

Dissolve the agar powder (It is important to use agar powder versus agar flakes as cooking times vary) in warm water. Place in a saucepan and bring to a boil. Cover and simmer on low for 4–5 minutes.

Transfer to a blender once the water/agar mixture has boiled the correct amount of time and add cashews. Blend on high for 1–2 minutes. Stir in lemon juice, nutritional yeast flakes, basil, salt, onion powder, garlic powder, dill weed, parsley, Chicken-style Seasoning, and chives.

Pour into a mold and chill. Use as a spread on bagels, toast or crackers.

MAKES: 3 cups

> **Tips/Comments**
>
> **For the Holidays try this:** After the schmear has set, shape it like a pinecone and then position roasted almonds on the top to resemble an authentic pine cone. Surround with crackers.

Guacamole

4 avocados
1 tablespoon **lemon juice**
1 teaspoon **onion powder**
1 teaspoon **garlic powder**
⅔ teaspoon **salt**
¼ cup **tomatoes**, chopped fine
2 pinches **cayenne pepper**, optional

Mash avocados until desired consistency, add lemon juice, onion powder, garlic powder, salt, tomatoes, and cayenne pepper, and stir thoroughly.

Chill. Add chopped onions and mayo, if desired.

MAKES: 1½ cups

> **Tips/Comments**
>
> "Avocados are sometimes called vegetable butter. Although they are around 70-80 percent fat, there is no cholesterol in avocados." (Roehl, Evelyn, *Whole Foods Facts,* p. 148).

Melty Cheese

½ large **red pepper** or 4 oz. **pimentos**
¼ cup **oatmeal**
½ cup **cashews**
1 teaspoon **onion powder**
½ cup **nutritional yeast flakes**
2 tablespoons **cornstarch**
2 tablespoons **lemon juice**
1½ teaspoons **salt**

Blend in a blender the red pepper, oatmeal, cashews, onion powder, nutritional yeast flakes, cornstarch, lemon juice, and salt with 1 cup hot water (adding gradually) until nuts disappear and the mixture is creamy smooth.

Heat 1½ cups water in a saucepan until it comes to a boil. Once the water is boiling, add the nut mixture to the boiling water. Stir constantly, about 2 minutes, until Melty Cheese is thickened.

Once the Melty Cheese has cooled down, I like to put it in a Ziploc® bag.. The corner can be snipped, and the cheese can be squeezed out onto whatever you are making.

MAKES: 3½ cups

Slicing Cheese

2 tablespoons **agar-agar powder**
1½ cups **cashews**
3 tablespoons **pimentos or red pepper**
¼ teaspoon **paprika**
3 tablespoons **nutritional yeast flakes**

3 tablespoons **lemon juice**
1 teaspoons **salt**
1 teaspoon **onion powder**
¼ teaspoon **garlic powder**

Dissolve the agar powder (It is important to use agar powder versus agar flakes as cooking times vary.) in 2 cups warm water. Place in a saucepan and bring to a boil. Cover and simmer on low for 4–5 minutes.

Transfer to a blender once the water /agar mixture has boiled the correct amount of time and add cashews, pimentos, and paprika. Blend on high for 1–2 minutes. Then add the nutritional yeast flakes, lemon juice, salt, onion powder, and garlic powder. Blend all ingredients thoroughly.

Pour into containers and chill till firm. Line the pan or mold with plastic wrap for easy removal.

Variation: Add ½ cup hot cooked millet to this recipe, for additional nutrition.

MAKES: 3 cups

> **Tips/Comments**
> This is a very soft cheese, something like Velveeta®. Things you can do with Slicing Cheese: Freeze and grate slicing cheese to use in your favorite recipe. Make Macaroni and Cheese with this recipe by simply leaving out the Agar Agar and adding it to 3–4 cups of cooked macaroni.

Soft Yellow Cheese-Like Spread

¼ cup **fresh lemon juice**
1 yellow **pepper or** ¼ cup **pimento**
3 tablespoons **soy sauce**

1 large **clove of garlic**
¾ cup **raw cashews**
⅓ cup **nutritional yeast flakes**

Blend lemon juice, pepper, soy sauce, garlic, cashews, and nutritional yeast flakes until smooth, a good minute.

Refrigerate and use within a couple of days. (It thickens as it stands.) This is great for dipping veggies in or topping Mexican food and casseroles.

MAKES: 1½ cups

Vegan Ricotta

1 pound **tofu (extra firm)**
1 cup **raw cashews**
1 cup **hot water**
1 tablespoon **lemon juice**
4 garlic **cloves**

½ teaspoon **salt**
1 tablespoon **basil**
1 tablespoon **oregano**
1 tablespoon **onion powder**
1 tablespoon **garlic powder**

Crumble tofu into a cottage cheese-like consistency in a large bowl. I also like to grate it up for even size pieces.

Blend cashews, hot water, lemon juice, and garlic, until smooth.

Pour over tofu and mix together. Add salt, basil, oregano, onion powder, and garlic powder. Mix well.

MAKES: 3 cups

Tips/Comments
For color and variety, add spinach, shredded carrots or other vegetables of choice. This goes well in Lasagna or in Stuffed Shells.

Corn Butter

1 teaspoon **agar-agar powder**
1 cup **cool water**
¼ cup **cornmeal**
¼ teaspoon **salt**
2 tablespoons **shredded carrots**

1½ teaspoons **lemon juice**
¼ cup **shredded coconut** (opt.)
½ cup **raw cashews**
¼ teaspoon **salt**
1 cup **warm water**

Dissolve agar-agar in cool water in a saucepan, and then add cornmeal; stir till free of lumps. Bring Agar, cornmeal, salt, and carrots to a boil.

Cook until thickened and carrots are soft, about 5 minutes.

Place lemon juice, coconut, cashews, salt, and warm water in a blender along with cooked cornmeal. Blend 2–3 minutes.

Pour into a mold and chill till firm.

MAKES: 2 cups

Tips/Comments
It might be better to call this Corn Spread. Whatever the case, we've come to really appreciate this moist and mild spread for a great, low-fat alternative to butter or margarine. Add garlic to it for garlic butter.

Date Butter

1 cup **pitted dates** cut in pieces
1 cup **boiling water**

Place dates and boiling water into a blender and blend on high for 2–3 minutes or until very smooth. You can add more or less water, depending on consistency desired.

Variations: ½ cup dates and ½ cup dried apples or apricots. Use as a spread for bread or as a substitution for margarine and sugar in sweet rolls.

MAKES: 1½ cups

Racy Ketchup

1 (12-ounce) **can tomato puree**, about 1⅓ cups
½ cup **tomato paste**
¼ teaspoon **oregano**
2 teaspoons **onion powder**
3 tablespoons **apple juice concentrate**
½ teaspoon **garlic powder**
2 tablespoons **lemon juice**
½–1 teaspoon **salt**
2 tablespoons **flax seed gel** (p. 108) or **olive oil**
½ teaspoon **basil**

Blend tomato puree, tomato paste, oregano, onion powder, juice concentrate, garlic powder, lemon juice, salt, flax seed gel or olive oil, and basil together well to get rid of lumps of seasonings. Keep refrigerated when not in use. This lasts 2 weeks.

Tips/Comments
For a spicy variation, add 1 tablespoon chili powder seasoning.

MAKES: 2½ cups

Tofu Mayonnaise

1 (12-ounce) **brick silken tofu**
2 cloves **garlic**
1 tablespoon **potato flour**
1 teaspoon **juice concentrate**
1 teaspoon **salt**
¼–⅓ cup **lemon juice**
1 tablespoon **nutritional yeast flakes**
1 tablespoon **chopped onion**

Blend in a blender the tofu, garlic, potato flour, juice concentrate, salt, lemon juice, nutritional yeast flakes, onion, and 1–3 tablespoons of water together until very smooth. Use more or less water, depending on what firmness of tofu you use or what thickness of mayonnaise you want.

MAKES: 1½ cups

Tofu Sour Cream

1 (12-ounce) **brick silken tofu**
½ teaspoon **salt**
1 tablespoon **lemon juice**
2 tablespoons **flax seed gel* or oil** (optional)
1½ teaspoon **apple juice concentrate** or **honey**

Blend tofu, salt, lemon juice, flax seed gel or oil, and juice concentrate or honey until smooth, chill and serve.

MAKES: 1½ cups

Cashew Gravy

*1 cup **cashews, raw**
Or ½ cup **cashews** & ½ cup **sunflower seeds**
3 tablespoons **soy sauce**
1 tablespoon **onion powder**
¼ cup **corn starch**
⅓ cup **Chicken-style Seasoning** (p. 64)
½ teaspoon **salt**, optional
1 tablespoon **nutritional yeast flakes**
1 cup **hot water**

Blend in a blender the cashews (and sunflower seeds, if using), soy sauce, onion powder, cornstarch, Chicken-style Seasoning, salt, and nutritional yeast flakes in hot water. Allow to blend for a few minutes. You want this to turn into a pasty substance.

Put 3 cups of water on to boil. When blended ingredients are pasty, add to boiling water and thicken by stirring constantly until it bubbles.

*May substitute Brazil nuts for cashews, to make Brazil Nut Gravy. (Great with mashed potatoes)

MAKES: 10 (½-cup) servings

Toasted Sunflower Seeds

4 cups **raw sunflower seeds**
¾ cup **soy sauce**

Rinse sunflower seeds in a large strainer. Drain.

Place rinsed sunflower seeds in a dry skillet and roast over medium-high heat until starting to brown.

Add soy sauce to roasted sunflower seeds, and continue to cook until the liquid is evaporated. When the liquid is gone from the sunflower seeds, remove from skillet and place on a slightly greased baking sheet. The skillet will look like a huge mess, but the cleanup is pretty easy—soap and water cleanup.

Bake at 350 degrees, turning every 2 minutes until completely dried out, about 10 minutes.

MAKES: 4 cups

Papaya Trail Mix

3 cups **raw almonds**, rinsed
1½ cups **raw sunflower seeds**, rinsed
1½ cups **raw pumpkin seeds**, rinsed
2½ cups **papaya**
2 cups **Craisins**®
2 cups **raisins**
¾ cup **carob chips**

Rinse and place the almonds on a cookie sheet and roast in a 350-degree oven for 10 minutes, stirring once. Rinse and place the pumpkin and sunflower seeds on a sprayed cookie sheet and follow the same direction as for the almonds.

Cool completely!! Once cooled add the papaya, Craisins®, raisins, and carob chips. Mix well and enjoy! I like this trail mix because it is not so sweet.

MAKES: 12 cups

> **Tips/Comments**
> Don't get put off by the word tofu. "Tofu is very high in protein, between 35–45 percent of calories per serving. Tofu contains a high amount of lysine, the amino acid in which most grains are deficient. Tofu can be an excellent source of calcium, iron, phosphorus, and B-complex vitamins." (Roehl, Evelyn, *Whole Foods Facts,* p. 6).

Egg Substitute

3 tablespoons **ground flax or chia seed**
1 cup **hot water**
1 tablespoon **olive oil**

Blend seeds and oil together in hot water until it is foamy. I use ¼ cup for a replacement of one egg. These substitutes give the binding properties of an egg but not the rising ability.

MAKES: 1¼ cups

> **Tips/Comments**
> Some use this mixture for a tea to soothe the intestines, but I like to use it as an oil replacement. Flax seeds are high in Omega 3 fatty acids, which boost the immune system and will significantly reduce cholesterol and triglyceride levels.

Seasonings

If you look at the label of the seasoning mixes in the supermarket, you may wonder, "Just what is this I'm putting into my body?"

Here's a simple solution to that, make your own seasoning mixes. They will only take a few minutes and taste wonderful!

Chicken-style Seasoning

1⅓ cups **nutritional yeast flakes**
1 teaspoon **celery seed**
3 tablespoons **onion powder**
2 tablespoons **Sucanat®**
2½ teaspoons **garlic powder**
2 tablespoons **Italian seasoning**
2 tablespoons **salt**
½ teaspoon **turmeric**

Blend nutritional yeast flakes, celery seed, onion powder, Sucanat®, garlic powder, Italian seasoning, salt, and turmeric, and stir in 2 tablespoons dried parsley.

This is great for a soup base and works well as a seasoning for other favorite dishes.

MAKES: 1½ cups

Mild Chili Seasoning

¼ cup **paprika**
¼ cup **cumin**
1½ tablespoons **oregano**
3 tablespoons **garlic powder**
1½ tablespoons **Italian Seasoning**
1 teaspoon **turmeric**

Blend paprika, cumin, oregano, garlic powder, Italian Seasoning, and turmeric on high until fine, stopping the blender 2–3 times to stir. Store in an airtight container, glass works best.

MAKES: ¾ cup

Country-Style Seasoning

2 cups **yeast flakes**
¾ teaspoon **turmeric**
1½ tablespoons **onion powder**
1½ teaspoons **dried parsley**
1 tablespoon **garlic powder**
1½ tablespoons **Sucanat®**
1½ tablespoons **paprika**
¼ cup **salt**
¾ teaspoon **celery seed**

Blend in a dry blender the yeast flakes, turmeric, onion powder, parsley, garlic powder, Sucanat®, paprika, salt, and celery seed on high until fine. Let blended mixture sit in the covered blender for a few seconds to allow powder dust to settle. Store in a dry covered container, glass is best.

MAKES: 1½ cups

Walnut Parmesan Cheese

1 cup **walnuts**
½ teaspoon **salt**
½ cup **nutritional yeast flakes**

Place walnuts, salt, and nutritional yeast flakes together in a blender. Blend to desired consistency.

MAKES: 1 cup

Parmesan-Like Topping

1 cup **white sesame seeds**
½ teaspoon **garlic powder**
2 teaspoons **salt**
2 tablespoons **Chicken-style Seasoning** (p. 64)
1 cup **nutritional yeast flakes**
2 tablespoons **lemon juice**
2 teaspoons **onion powder**

Toast sesame seeds on medium-high in a dry skillet, stirring constantly until slightly browned and beginning to crackle.

Remove from heat and blend on high until finely ground.

Pour into a bowl and add garlic powder, salt, Chicken-style Seasoning, nutritional yeast flakes, lemon juice, and onion powder, mixing together well with hands. Keep refrigerated.

MAKES: 1¾ cups.

Breading Meal

2 cups **whole wheat flour** *(for wheat free, use brown rice flour)
¼ cup **dried parsley**
1 cup **nutritional yeast flakes**
1 tablespoon **garlic powder**
1 tablespoon **salt**
1 cup **cornmeal**

Put flour, parsley, yeast flakes, garlic powder, salt, and cornmeal in a bowl and stir together well. This is a great breading for Eggplant Parmesan or any of your other breading needs. I like to make a batch and store it in the freezer to be used as I need.

MAKES: 4 cups

Pesto

4 cups **lightly packed fresh basil**
4 cups **lightly packed fresh parsley**
1 teaspoon **salt**
4 garlic **cloves**
½ cup **olive oil**
¼ cup **pine nuts**

Remove large, coarse stems from basil and parsley and discard.

Using the "S" blade, place parsley and basil leaves in a food processor. Process for a few minutes.

Now add salt, garlic, pine nuts, and olive oil to the processor, and process for 2 minutes. Put any unused Pesto in a container and freeze for future use.

MAKES: 1 cup

Sweet Chile Sauce (Sweet & Sour Sauce)

3/4 cup **honey**
3/4 cup **salsa**
1½ cups **lemon juice**
1 tablespoon **cornstarch**

Place honey, lemon juice, salsa, and cornstarch in a blender. Blend for 1–2 minutes.

Pour blended mixture in a saucepan and thicken.

This is a wonderful sweet & sour sauce that goes well over Spring Rolls (p. 31).

MAKES: 3 cups

Sides

Kale with Tomatoes

1 bunch **of kale, about 8 large leaves**
1 small **onion**, chopped
¾ cup **diced tomatoes**
Salt to taste, optional

Wash kale and remove the stocks from the leaves. Chop kale into 2-inch pieces, set aside.

Sauté onion in a small amount of water or cooking oil, add tomatoes, and pile the kale on top of tomatoes and onions.

Cover your pan and let kale wilt down to a manageable size. Simmer for a few minutes. Mix together and serve.

SERVES: 6

> **Tips/Comments**
> You may add seasoned Baked Tofu 2 (page 43) to this dish for added flavor.

Twice-baked Potatoes

4 medium **potatoes**
12 tablespoons **cashew or soy milk**
4 large teaspoons **corn butter**
Salt to **taste**

Bake potatoes until tender, about one hour at 350 degrees.

Scoop out contents and mash with cashew milk, corn butter, and salt to taste. Add parsley if desired. Top with a sprinkle of paprika.

Broil until slightly browned and crispy.

To add a little zip to your potatoes try this:

½ cup **Tofutti® Sour Cream**
2 tablespoons **Vegenaise®**
1 teaspoon **granulated onion**
1 teaspoon **salt (I like Vege-Sal®)**
½ cup **chopped broccoli**
¼ cup **chopped onion**
½ cup **sliced or chopped olives**

Bake potatoes until tender, about one hour at 350 degrees. Cut in half and hollow out the potato centers.

Mash potato centers and add the sour cream, Vegenaise®, granulated onion, and salt. Mix this together and if you would like it a little creamier, add a little soy milk.

Sauté or lightly steam broccoli and onion.

Now mix potato mixture and veggies together. Fill the potato skins with mixture and place in a hot oven for an additional 10 minutes.

Melty Cheese (p. 57) is another tasty addition to top potatoes with.

SERVES: 8

Fried Rice

2½ cups **raw brown rice**
5 cups **water**
1 cup **frozen peas**
½ cup **chopped carrots**
½ cup **chopped celery**
1 small **onion**, chopped
½ cup **Chicken-style Seasoning** (p. 64)

Sauté rice in a dry skillet on medium heat by stirring constantly until lightly browned. After rice is sautéed, add water and cook for 50 minutes. I like the rice to be well done but if you like it a little chewy, shorten the cooking time to 40 minutes.

Chop carrots, celery, and onion, and sauté them in a small amount of water or olive oil while rice is cooking. When rice and veggies are done, combine along with Chicken-style Seasoning. You can place this in a casserole dish and reheat if need be or serve immediately.

SERVES: 10

Greek Green Beans

¼ small **red onion**, coarsely chopped
1 garlic **clove**, pressed
1 tablespoon **olive oil or water**
1 cup **diced tomatoes**
1 pound **frozen green beans**
½ cup **sliced pitted ripe olives**
½ teaspoon **oregano**
¼ pound **Tofu Feta Cheese** (p. 86)

Sauté onion and garlic in olive oil or water. Add tomatoes, oregano, green beans and olives.

Cover and heat until green beans are hot, stirring every few minutes.

Place in a serving dish and sprinkle with Tofu Feta Cheese.

SERVES: 6

Spinach with Tofu

1 pound **firm tofu**, cut into cubes
3 tablespoons **Chicken-style Seasoning** (p. 64)
2 tablespoons **olive oil**
3 tablespoons **tamari or soy sauce**
½ teaspoon **cumin seeds**
½ small **red onion**, diced
1 garlic **clove**, crushed
1 pound **fresh baby spinach**
1 teaspoon **salt or Vege-Sal®**

Mix oil, Chicken-style Seasoning, and tamari together well. Pour over cubed tofu and allow to marinate for 10 minutes.

Place in a single layer on a sprayed baking pan and bake at 350 degrees for 30 minutes or until slightly crispy.

Stir cumin seeds in a hot fry pan to toast. Add onions, garlic, and a small amount of olive oil.

Sauté together for a few minutes. Add spinach and salt, toss.

Cover and cook for 3 minutes. Stir in tofu and continue to cook for 1 more minute.

Serve hot.

SERVES: 6

Calico Corn

2 tablespoons **olive oil**
Pinch **red pepper flakes**
½ **green pepper**, coarsely chopped
½ **red pepper**, coarsely chopped
½ red **onion**, coarsely chopped
1 small **carrot**, julienned
4 cups **frozen corn**
1 teaspoon **Vege-Sal®**

Place olive oil in a large frying pan, sprinkle in red pepper flakes, and sauté with peppers, onions, and carrots. Add the corn, sprinkle in Vege-Sal®.

Cook covered on medium heat for a few minutes. Stir several times and heat completely.

SERVES: 8

Garlic/Oregano Sweet Potatoes

3 **sweet potatoes or yams**
2 tablespoons **pumpkin seeds**
2 sprigs **fresh oregano**
1 **garlic clove**, crushed

½ teaspoon **salt**
1 teaspoon **lemon juice**
1 tablespoon **olive oil**

Cube sweet potatoes (or yams) and place in a medium bowl. Add pumpkin seeds, oregano, garlic, salt, lemon juice and olive oil, toss together.

Spread evenly on a baking sheet and bake at 350 degrees for 40 minutes.

SERVES: 6

Spanish Rice

2 cups **long grain brown rice**
½ **onion**, chopped
2 stalks **celery**
½ green **pepper**, chopped
1¼ cups **diced tomatoes**
2 cups **frozen corn**

1¼ cups **sliced black olives**
1 teaspoon **salt**
1 teaspoon **garlic powder**
2 teaspoons **onion powder**
½ tablespoon **cumin**
2 teaspoons **chili powder**

Rinse rice (optional). Place in a saucepan with 4 cups of water (You may toast in a dry frying pan before placing in boiling water to dextrinize the rice).

Bring to a boil. Reduce heat and cover. Rice takes about 45 minutes to cook.

Sauté onions, celery, and peppers in a large skillet. Toss in tomatoes, corn, and black olives. Add salt, garlic powder, onion powder, cumin, and chili powder. Bring to a bubble and add cooked rice. This can be served right away or placed in a casserole dish and bake at 350 degrees for 20 minutes. (Baking is optional)

SERVES: 8

Roasted Root Vegetables

1 **potato**
1 sweet **potato**
2 small **carrots**
½ red **onion**
½ red **pepper**
1 tablespoon **oil**
Other root **vegetables of your choice**
  (**parsnips, turnips, rutabaga, squash or beets**)
¼ teaspoon **rosemary**
¼ teaspoon **thyme**
¼ teaspoon **Vege-Sal®**
A pinch **of parsley**
A pinch **of dill**

Cube the potato, sweet potato, carrots, onion, red pepper, and any other vegetables of your choice into ½-inch cubes. Place vegetables into a medium sized mixing bowl.

Drizzle the oil over the veggies and toss together. Add the rosemary, thyme, Vege-Sal®, parsley, and dill, and toss again.

Bake at 375 degrees for 35 minutes, turning once during the baking process.

SERVES: 6

Spinach/Fennel Yams (or Sweet Potatoes)

3 medium **yams or sweet potatoes**
2 tablespoons **olive oil**
½ tablespoon **fennel seeds**
6 cups **fresh spinach leaves**

Scrub the potatoes and cut into cubes.

Heat oil and fennel seeds in a large skillet, allow fennel to slightly brown.

Add yams (or sweet potatoes) to skillet along with a small amount of water. Cover. Cook on medium heat until yams are soft when poked with a fork.

Add the spinach on top of the yams or sweet potatoes and let wilt. Once the spinach has wilted, mix together and serve.

SERVES: 6

Scalloped Potatoes

4 cups **raw potatoes, sliced thinly***
½ cup **raw cashews**
1 teaspoon **salt**
1 tablespoon **nutritional yeast flakes**
½ teaspoon **onion powder**
½ teaspoon **garlic powder**
½ teaspoon **basil**
½ teaspoon **cumin and/or sage**
½ cup **hot water**
3½ cups **water** (now or later, you choose)

*To speed up this process, you may slice the potatoes, and then blanch them in the three and a half cups of water.

Blend in a blender the cashews, salt, nutritional yeast flakes, and onion powder using ½ cup very hot water until cashews are smooth and disappear (about 1 minute). Add 3½ more cups of water to the blender if you did not blanch potatoes. If there is leftover water from the blanching, add that to the blended cashews.

Stir in the basil, cumin, and sage (if using both) once the cashew mixture is blended.

Place potatoes in a sprayed baking dish and pour blended liquid over potatoes.

Cover with foil and bake at 375 degrees for 1–1½ hours. You may want to uncover the dish for the last 10 minutes. Sprinkle with paprika when ready to serve.

SERVES: 8

Cajun Style Polenta with Mushrooms

1¼ cups **water**
½ teaspoon **salt**
½ teaspoon **granulated onion**
¼ teaspoon **paprika**
⅛ teaspoon **cayenne**
⅛ teaspoon **oregano**
1 cup **cornmeal**
¾ cup **cold water**

Bring water to boil over high heat in a heavy saucepan. Add salt, granulated onion, paprika, cayenne, and oregano to the boiling water.

Mix the cornmeal and ¾ cup cold water together in a small bowl and slowly add to the boiling water. Bring this mixture to a boil then reduce heat to low, cover and cook for 15–20 minutes stirring often.

Spoon fully cooked cornmeal (polenta) onto a greased cookie sheet in two-inch circles that are ½-inch thick. Cool. Or you can place in a mold, cool, and then slice.

Preheat oven to 400 degrees. Place polenta on greased cookie sheet and lightly grease the top of the polenta. Bake until polenta is lightly browned, about 15 minutes.

Topping

⅛–¼ cup **olive oil or water**
½ small **onion**, half moons
1 large **garlic clove**, crushed or minced
1 pound **button mushrooms**, sliced
¼ cup **red pepper**, diced
1 teaspoon **dried basil**
1 tablespoon **fresh parsley**, chopped

Heat the oil or water in a large skillet, and add onion, garlic, mushrooms, red pepper, basil, and parsley. Cook until mushrooms and onions are tender.

When polenta and mushroom mixture is ready, place polenta on plates, and top with a spoonful of mushrooms. Garnish with a sprig of parsley.

SERVES: 8

Asparagus Bruschetta

1 loaf **bruschetta bread**
6 garlic **cloves, minced**
2 tablespoons **shallots or leek rings**
½ teaspoon **salt** to taste
½ teaspoon **cayenne** or to taste
1½ teaspoons **lemon juice**
1 teaspoon **tamari**
1½ pounds of **asparagus**
¼ cup **water**

Sauté garlic, shallots or leeks in a small amount of oil or water. Add salt, cayenne, lemon juice, tamari, asparagus, and water.

Cover and reduce heat on asparagus mixture. Cook for about 5 minutes or until asparagus is to the desired tenderness.

Slice bruschetta bread and lightly toast.

Place toast on plates and top with 5 or 6 asparagus pieces on the side and drizzle a small amount of the garlic, shallot or leek juice on top.

SERVES: 8

Green Bean Bundles

8–10 whole **green beans** for each bundle
A couple of **carrot sticks** the length of your green beans for each bundle
A couple of **red pepper slices** for each bundle

Optional:
Summer squash sticks
Zucchini sticks
Green onions
Leek strips
¼ teaspoon **thyme**
¼ teaspoon **dill**
1 tablespoon **salt**

Use a layer of leek, torn into strips to tie your bundles together; I suggest a tie at each end of the bundle.

Bring two inches of water to a boil in a large skillet, adding the thyme, dill, and salt. Place each bundle in the boiling water, cover and boil for 5 minutes, turning once.

Remove each bundle carefully and place on a greased cookie sheet.

Brush each bundle with a small amount of oil and bake at 350 degrees for 5 more minutes. Serve while bundles are hot.

SERVES: 8 to 10

Salads

Sprouting

It may take a little extra effort to sprout your lentils, but it will be well worth the effort. To sprout lentils, soak them overnight. The next morning rinse them and leave them moist. Rinse morning and evening for three days and you will have a tasty addition to your bread and to salads.

You can sprout other grains and seeds such as alfalfa seeds, broccoli seeds, garbanzo beans, and many other seeds and nuts you can find in your local health food store. Almonds take on a whole different flavor and texture if soaked in water overnight. Tasty!!!

*I don't recommend sprouting black beans.

Greek "Feta" Salad

1 pound **water packed tofu**
2 teaspoons **onion powder**
½ teaspoon **garlic powder**
1 teaspoon **salt**
2 tablespoons **olive oil**
2 tablespoons **lemon juice**
1 **yellow & 1 red pepper**, cut into rings
1 cup **Greek olives**
1 small **red onion**, cut into rings
1 **cucumber**, cut into half moons
2 cups **grape tomatoes**
1 head **Romaine lettuce**, torn
2 cups **fresh spinach**

Start by crumbling tofu in a small bowl. Sprinkle with onion powder, garlic powder, salt, olive oil, and lemon juice. Mix together well; divide into three parts and set aside until needed. This is referred to as "Tofu mixture" in this recipe.

In a large salad bowl, begin making layers. A thin layer of Romaine and spinach torn into bite-sized pieces, a thin layer of peppers, a thin layer of onions, a thin layer of olives, a thin layer of cucumbers, a thin layer of tomatoes, and a thin layer of "Tofu mixture."

To complete the salad, do this layering two more times. Dressing for this salad is found on page 91 (Greek "Feta" Salad Dressing).

SERVES: 8

Leafy Green Fruit Salad

- 4 cups **lettuce/spinach/salad greens**, packed
- ¼ cup **slivered almonds/pecans/or your choice of nut**
- ¼ cup of **shredded carrots**
- 1 **apple**, diced
- ½ small can of **mandarin oranges**
- ¼ cup **dried cranberries**
- ¼ cup **red onion rings**
- ½ cup **sliced strawberries**
- ½ to **1 cup raspberry style dressing**

Toss together the greens, nuts, carrots, apple, oranges, cranberries, onion rings, strawberries, and dressing, and serve right away. When making ahead of time, leave dressing off until right before serving.

SERVES: 6

Red Tip Lettuce Salad

- 1 head **red tip lettuce**
- 12 **cherry tomatoes**
- 3 ounces **alfalfa sprouts**

Tear lettuce into bite size pieces, slice cherry tomatoes in half and pull apart sprouts.

Toss together in a large bowl for a colorful and nutritious salad.

Taco Salad Bowls

It can be easy to make your own Taco Salad bowls, and you don't have to deep-fry them! Using whole wheat tortillas, moisten them by running them under water and shaking off the excess. Place oven safe bowls upside down on a baking sheet, lightly spray the outside, and place a tortilla on each one. You will want to use small bowls, so your tortilla hangs down in a bowl shape. Lightly brown your "bowls" in a 350-degree oven 15–20 minutes. Now fill your tortilla bowls with things like Spanish rice, beans, lettuce, salsa, tomato pieces, Melty Cheese, green onions, and black olives. Let your imagination lead you.

SERVES: 6

Ten Layer Bean Salad

2 cups **cooked rice**, optional, plain or seasoned
You can season your rice with:
- 1 teaspoon **chili powder**
- ½ teaspoon **onion powder**
- ¼ teaspoon **cumin**

4 cups **pinto beans or black beans** or mix of both
2 cups **corn, frozen or freshly cut off the cob**
4 cups **chopped lettuce, iceberg, Romaine or other leaf lettuce**
1½ cups **salsa**, your favorite kind
2 cups **cheese, Daiya® or your favorite nut cheese*
1 cup **sour cream, Toffuti®***
1 cup **guacamole***
1 to 2 cups **chopped tomatoes**
1 cup **sliced black olives**
½ cup **chopped green onions**

Layer in a 9x13-inch pan the ingredients in the order listed: rice, beans, corn, lettuce, salsa, cheese, sour cream, guacamole, tomatoes, olives, and onions.

Cut into sections once everything is layered and serve over crushed Fritos.

If you omit the lettuce, this can double as a 10-layer dip, served with corn chips. (Blue corn chips make for a great color contrast.) If you want to make this real simple for yourself, you can use quick brown rice, canned beans that are rinsed, a small bag of frozen corn and 2 small cans of olives, to save yourself from measuring these items out.

*The following salad recipes are wonderful stand-alone salads. However, I recommend serving them on a bed of greens such as Romaine, spinach, iceberg, spring mix or any other greens that you like. These are tasty dressing substitutes.

SERVES: 8

Tips/Comments

I have found that an easy way to spread nut cheese, sour cream, guacamole or any liquid type substance, is to put it in a baggie and snip a small corner off the bag and squeeze out the substance in the places you want it. Putting it on with a spoon just seems to make big clumps. This way you can have smaller sections without the big clumps.

Carrot Salad

4 cups **carrots**, shredded
½ cup **raisins**
¼ cup **walnuts**, chopped
1 cup **Vegenaise**®

Mix carrots, raisins, and walnuts in a large mixing bowl. Add Vegenaise®. Mix all ingredients together and place in a serving bowl.

MAKES: 8 (½-cup) servings

> **Tips/Comments**
> This is a salad I learned to make from my mother. I remember it as a child when she used to make homemade mayonnaise, something I no longer do. But if you have a favorite mayonnaise recipe, you may use it instead of Vegenaise®.

Barley, Corn, and Pepper Salad

1 cup **uncooked pearl barley**
2½ cups **water**
2 cups **frozen corn**, thawed & drained
½ cup **diced red bell pepper**
½ cup **diced green bell pepper**
½ cup **sliced green onion**

Cook barley in boiling water for 40–50 minutes. Rinse to cool and drain.

Combine in a large bowl the cooked barley, corn, peppers, and onions along with Cilantro Dressing (see next recipe), toss well. Serve while warm or chill.

SERVES: 8

Cilantro Dressing

⅓ cup **flax seed gel** (p. 108) or oil
¼ cup **chopped fresh cilantro**
⅓ cup **lemon juice**
½ teaspoon **salt**
½ teaspoon **Spike**®

Blend flax seed gel (or oil), cilantro, lemon juice, salt, and Spike® for 30–45 seconds in a blender.

Pour over Barley Corn Salad and toss to combine.

MAKES: ¾ cup

Creamy Tofu Cottage Cheese

⅔ cup **raw cashews**
⅛ teaspoon **garlic powder**
1 teaspoon **salt**
1 tablespoon **nutritional yeast flakes**
½ teaspoon **onion powder**
1½ tablespoon **lemon juice**
1 pound **crumbled tofu**

Blend in a blender the cashews, garlic powder, salt, nutritional yeast flakes, onion powder, and lemon juice with ½ cup hot water.

Stir in tofu. Add chopped tomatoes, parsley, onion, etc. if desired.

SERVES: 4

> **Tips/Comments**
>
> You might want to try this in a stuffed tomato. Core and cut your tomato into eighths, not cutting the tomato completely apart by *not* severing the bottom. Stuff with "Creamy Cottage Cheese" and sprinkle with paprika, parsley, or chives.

Wild Rice Salad

2 cups **wild rice**
4 cups **water**
¼ cup **Chicken-style Seasoning** (p. 64)
1 cup **roasted almonds**
½ cup **chopped red pepper**
½ cup **diced carrots**
½ cup **chopped green pepper**
½ cup **chopped red onion**

Cook rice in water about 45 minutes, or until done to the consistency you prefer. Cool.

Toss together Chicken-style Seasoning, almonds, red and green peppers, carrots, and onion and chill. This is a very colorful and delicious salad.

SERVES: 8

Sprout Salad

1 package **bean or alfalfa sprouts (4–5 ounces)**
1 stalk **celery, chopped fine**
¼ red **onion, minced**
¼ cup **sunflower seeds, raw or roasted**

You may use any type of sprout desired: lentil, adzuki or any sprouted grain.

Toss together with celery, onion, sunflower seeds, and your favorite dressing. Or make garlic dressing.

Garlic Dressing

3 cloves **crushed garlic**
½ cup **lemon juice**
¼ cup **flax seed gel** (p. 108) or oil

Whiz garlic, lemon juice, and flax gel or oil together in a blender for 30 seconds and pour over sprout mixture.

Quinoa Salad

1½ cups **quinoa**
3 cups **water**
3 green **onions**, chopped
1 large **red pepper**, diced
1 large **avocado**, diced
1 cup **black beans**, cooked

¼ cup **fresh parsley**, chopped
¼ cup **cilantro**, chopped
1 tablespoon **Spike®**
½ teaspoon **cumin**
¼ cup **lemon juice (or lime juice)**
1 tablespoon **lemon or lime zest**

Place rinsed quinoa in a saucepan and cover with water. Bring to a boil, and cook for 20 minutes. After the quinoa is cooked, cool while preparing the raw vegetables.

Toss onions, pepper, avocado, beans, parsley, cilantro, Spike®, cumin, and lemon juice together with cooked quinoa, mix well. This may be served warm or cold.

SERVES: 10

Tips/Comments

For a completely raw salad, you may sprout the quinoa for 10–12 hours. When sprouted, it will look like each quinoa has a little tail like a polliwog.

Garlic Ginger Coleslaw

1 head **Chinese (Napa) cabbage**
1 **red pepper** cut into rings
1 **green pepper** cut into rings
1 **yellow pepper** cut into rings
1 small **red onion** cut into rings
3 stalks of **celery** cut into crests

Slice Chinese cabbage VERY thin, place in a large bowl. After cutting the onion, celery, and peppers, mix in with cabbage.

Pour dressing (recipe below) over the salad mixture and stir until mixed nicely.

This is best if it is served right away. If you would like to make this ahead of time, just wait till it is time to serve before adding the dressing.

Dressing

¾ cup **olive oil**
½ cup **fresh lemon juice**
3 tablespoons **soy sauce**
2 tablespoons **maple syrup**
¼ cup **diced fresh ginger**
¼ cup **cashew butter***
⅓ cup **chopped fresh garlic**
½ teaspoon **salt**

Blend oil, lemon juice, soy sauce, maple syrup, ginger, butter, garlic, and salt together in a blender. Allow the blender to run for 1–2 minutes to make a very smooth dressing.

Pour over the above salad mixture and stir to coat.

SERVES: 10

> **Tips/Comments**
> You can use any kind of nut butter. Just keep in mind that something like peanut butter or tahini is strong enough to make the entire salad taste like them.

For the Birds Salad

1 cup **millet**
2 cups **water**
½ **wild rice**
1 cup **toasted sunflower seeds**
1½ cups **broccoli**, chopped
1 red **pepper**, chopped
1 cup **carrots**, shredded
1 small **red onion**, chopped
1½ cups **Mystery Dressing** (p. 92)

Bring water to a boil, 2 cups in 1 pan and 1 cup in another pan.

Place millet in the 2 cups of water and rice in the 1 cup of water.

Cook millet for 20 minutes and wild rice for 55 minutes. Cool both.

Mix cooled millet, wild rice, sunflower seeds, pepper, onion, broccoli, and carrots together in a large bowl. Now mix in Mystery Dressing and serve.

SERVES: 8

Autumn Salad

4 cups **cooked white beans**
1 **cucumber**, thinly sliced
4 **tomatoes**, diced
½ **red pepper**, diced
8 cups **frozen corn**, rinsed
1 small can **sliced black olives**

Lemonette Dressing

1 tablespoon **mustard**
½ cup **olive oil**
2 tablespoons **crushed garlic**
2 tablespoons **soy sauce (tamari)**
1 cup **fresh lemon juice**
1 teaspoon **Spike®**

Combine, beans, cucumber, tomatoes, pepper, corn, and black olives in a medium bowl. Stir together and notice the incredible color combination.

Blend and pour Lemonette Dressing over the top of corn mixture, mix, and allow salad to marinate for 30 minutes. It is best to chill during marinating time. Remix and serve.

SERVES: 8

Spring Pasta Salad

2 cups **bow tie pasta**
1 cup **baby spinach**, packed
2 **green onions**, tops & all, chopped
1 **tomato**, chopped
1 cup **frozen peas, rinsed**
1 tablespoon **fresh basil leaves**, minced or 1 tablespoon **Pesto**

1 tablespoon **olive oil**
1 **garlic clove**, pressed
1 teaspoon **Spike**®
¼ pound **of "Feta"** (see below)

Cook pasta according to package directions, rinse and cool. Sprinkle with a pinch of salt and mix.

Mix spinach, onions, tomato, peas, basil or Pesto, olive oil, garlic, and Spike® together in a large bowl while pasta cools. When thoroughly mixed together, add the cooked pasta. Toss together until pasta & spinach are evenly coated with seasonings. Complete by adding "Feta" to the salad.

SERVES: 10

Instructions for making "Feta."

1 pound **water packed extra firm tofu**
2 teaspoons **onion powder**
½ teaspoon **garlic powder**

1 teaspoon **salt**
2 tablespoons **olive oil**
2 tablespoons **lemon juice**

Crumble (I like to grate the tofu instead of crumbling) tofu in a small bowl.

Sprinkle with onion powder, garlic powder, salt, olive oil, and lemon juice.

Mix together well, set aside till needed. There will be extra "feta" that you can use for other salads. Or use extra in Garlic "Feta" Dressing (p. 90), Greek Green Beans (p. 69) or to make a small batch of Vegan Ricotta (p. 59). There are lots of different ways to use the extra "Feta."

Avocado Pasta Salad

2 cups **spiral pasta**
1 tablespoon **olive oil**
¼ cup **Honey Lemon Marinade** (p. 88)
1½ teaspoons **Spike**®

2 fresh **tomatoes**, diced
2 **green onions**, chopped, tops and all
½ **red pepper**, diced
1 **avocado**, diced

Cook pasta according to package directions, rinse and cool. Sprinkle with a pinch of salt and olive oil, and mix.

Coat the cooked pasta with Honey Lemon Marinade and Spike®. Mix in chopped tomatoes, onions, and pepper. Gently fold in the avocado last. Chill and serve.

SERVES: 8

Carrot and Nut Coleslaw

1 **carrot**, grated
1 small **red onion**, finely sliced half-moons
2 **celery stalks**, sliced
1 small **white cabbage or Napa Cabbage**, shredded
2 tablespoons **fresh parsley**, chopped

½ tablespoon **Spike®**
1 tablespoon **poppy seeds**
2 tablespoons **toasted sesame oil**
2 tablespoons **lemon juice**
¾ cup **cashews**, toasted

Combine the carrot, onion, celery, and cabbage in a large bowl.

Stir in the chopped parsley and season with Spike®. If you would like to add a toasted flavor to the poppy seed, heat poppy seeds in a dry skillet until they pop. Cool.

Add to veggies along with toasted sesame oil, lemon juice and cooled cashews. Toss together and serve.

SERVES: 8

Pesto Pasta Salad

4 cups **bow tie pasta**
½ cup **julienne carrots**
¾ cup **chopped broccoli**
3 chopped **green onions**
1 cup **frozen peas**, rinsed
1 cup **cherry tomatoes**
1 tablespoon **fresh lemon juice**

¼ cup **Pesto sauce** (p. 66)
2 tablespoons **olive oil**
¼ cup **Italian Dressing**
1 teaspoon **sage**
1 teaspoon **Spike®** (p. 116)
1 tablespoon **basil**

Cook pasta according to package directions. Cool.

Place in a large bowl and add carrots, broccoli, onions, peas, tomatoes, lemon juice, Pesto sauce, olive oil, Italian Dressing (Any favorite Italian Dressing can be used on the Pesto Pasta Salad dressing or it can be replaced by "Cheesy" Dijon Salad Dressing.), sage, Spike®, and basil. Toss together until well mixed, careful not to break the pasta. Serve.

SERVES: 10

Spicy Southern Pasta

1½ cups **spiral pasta**
1 tablespoon **olive oil**
½ cup **black olives**
½ small **red onion**, cut into half moons
½ **green pepper**, cut into short strips
1 **tomato**, cubed
1 **garlic clove**, crushed
1 tablespoon **fresh cilantro**
1 tablespoon **fresh basil**
¼ teaspoon **oregano**
1 pinch **red pepper flakes**
¾ teaspoon **salt**
¼ teaspoon **garlic granules**
1 or **2 pinches chili powder**
1 pinch of **cumin**

Cook pasta according to package directions, drain and rinse with cold water Mix in oil.

Place olives, onions, pepper, tomato, garlic, cilantro, basil, oregano, red pepper flakes, garlic granules, chili powder, and cumin in a large bowl and toss together. Add pasta.

Chill and serve.

SERVES: 10

Cauliflower Pea Salad

1 small head **cauliflower**
2 cups **frozen peas**
1 small **red pepper**
1 small **red onion**
1 teaspoon **onion powder**
1 teaspoon **salt**
¼ teaspoon **garlic powder**
1 to 2 cups **Vegenaise®**
½ cups **Tofutti® Sour Cream**
1 diced **avocado**

Cut the cauliflower into bite-sized pieces and place in large bowl. Rinse frozen peas in a colander under warm water and add to cauliflower.

Add chopped red pepper, chopped red onion, and mix with cauliflower and peas. Sprinkle cauliflower and veggies with garlic powder, onion powder, and salt. Toss together.

Mix the Vegenaise® (depending how much moisture you want in your salad, will depend on how much you use) and sour cream with the veggies until all is coated with dressing.

Add avocado chunks last, mixing softly to keep from crushing the avocado and spoon into a serving dish. Serve chilled.

SERVES: 10

Royal Coleslaw

1 head **purple cabbage**
4 **tomatoes**, diced

Shred cabbage, very fine, and place in a large bowl. Add tomatoes and mix together.

Prepare the dressing below and pour over the top of cabbage mixture and stir until mixed nicely. This is best if it is served right away. If you would like to make this ahead of time, just wait till it is time to serve before adding the dressing.

Dressing

¾ cup **olive oil**
½ cup **fresh lemon juice**
3 tablespoons **soy sauce**
2 tablespoons **maple syrup**
¼ cup **diced fresh ginger**

¼ cup **cashew butter***
⅓ cup **chopped fresh garlic**
½ teaspoon **salt**
2 avocados, **diced**

Blend oil, lemon juice, soy sauce, maple syrup, ginger, cashew butter, garlic, and salt together in a blender. Allow blender to run for 1–2 minutes to make a very smooth dressing.

Pour over the salad mixture and stir to coat. Add the avocados last so that you can fold them in without mushing them.

SERVES: 10

Tips/Comments

You can use any kind of nut butter just keep in mind that something like peanut butter or tahini is strong enough to make the entire salad taste like them.

Creamy Garlic Salad Dressing

1 cup **cashews, raw**
1 tablespoon **chopped onion**
1 tablespoon **garbanzo bean flour**
3 cloves **garlic**
1½ teaspoons **salt**
1 teaspoon **pineapple juice concentrate or honey**
1 teaspoon **nutritional yeast flakes**
¼ cup **lemon juice**

Blend in a blender the cashews, onion, flour, garlic, salt, pineapple juice or honey, nutritional yeast flakes, and lemon juice thoroughly with 1¼ hot cup water. You may add up to ¾ cup more water if you want the dressing to be thinner. If desired, stir in up to 1 cup crumbled tofu that has been liberally sprinkled with garlic powder, salt, and lemon juice. Another option would be to stir in 1 cup of diced avocado.

MAKES: 2 cups

French Dressing

1 cup **flax seed gel** (p. 108) or **olive oil**
¾ cup **tomato puree**
⅓ cup **lemon juice**
1 tablespoon **onion powder**
½ teaspoon **garlic powder**
1 tablespoon **paprika**
1 teaspoon **salt**
2 tablespoons **honey**

Blend flax seed or olive oil, tomato puree, lemon juice, onion powder, garlic powder, paprika, salt, and honey together on high, for 30–45 seconds.

Chill in a covered container. Dressing will last up to 2 weeks but serve within a week for premium freshness.

MAKES: 2½ cups

Creamy Ranch Dressing

1 cup **raw cashews**
1 teaspoon **garlic powder**
1 tablespoon **potato flour**
1 teaspoon **salt**
1 tablespoon **chopped onion**
2 tablespoons **lemon juice**
1 tablespoon **pineapple juice concentrate**
2 more **tablespoons of lemon juice**
1 tablespoon **basil**
1 teaspoon **dill weed**
1 teaspoon **Chicken-style Seasoning*** (p. 64)

Blend in a blender the cashews, garlic powder, potato flour, salt, onion, lemon juice, and pineapple juice concentrate with 1¼ cups water until creamy. Add up to ½ cup additional water to get desired consistency.

Stir in basil, dill weed, and Chicken-style Seasoning. Chill. Serve within a week for premium freshness.

MAKES: about 2 cups

Honey Lemon Marinade

2 cups **lemon juice**, fresh is best
2 teaspoons **salt**
1 cup **honey**
1½ teaspoons **granulated garlic**
1 tablespoon **granulated onion**

Blend lemon juice, salt, honey, garlic, and onion together and use as a dressing on your favorite salad.

MAKES: 3 cups

Tahini Blue Cheese Dressing

10 ounces **firm silken tofu**
1 teaspoon **dill weed**
Pinch of **paprika or cayenne pepper**
½ cup **non-dairy milk (soy)**
1 teaspoon **salt**
3 **garlic cloves**
2 teaspoons **onion powder**
⅓ cup **tahini**
½ cup **lemon juice**

Cut tofu brick in half and grate up one of the halves. Stir the dill weed and paprika or cayenne pepper into the grated tofu. Set aside.

Place milk, salt, garlic, onion powder, tahini, and lemon juice in a blender along with the remaining tofu and blend until very smooth. Stir in grated tofu mixture. Serve within a week for premium freshness.

MAKES: 2 cups

Greek "Feta" Salad Dressing

¾ cup **fresh lemon juice**
2 tablespoons **chopped red onion**
¼ cup **water** (hot)
2 tablespoons **honey**
½ cup **olive oil**
½ teaspoon **salt**
3 **garlic cloves**
2 pinches of **red pepper flakes**
2 teaspoons of **Pizza Seasoning** (p. 122)

Place lemon juice, onion, water, honey, olive oil, salt, garlic, red pepper flakes, and Pizza Seasoning in a blender, blending for about a minute.

Pour into a serving container and mix in shredded tofu, if desired.

MAKES: 1½ cups

"Cheesy" Dijon Salad Dressing

¼ pound **tofu**
⅓ cup **lemon juice**
⅓ cup **raw cashews**
2 tablespoons **chopped onion**
1 small **tomato**
½ teaspoon **salt**

1 tablespoon **soy sauce**
2 tablespoons **apple juice concentrate**
½ teaspoon **turmeric**
2 tablespoons **nutritional yeast flakes** (p. 116)
1 tablespoon **chives**
2 teaspoons **dill weed**

Blend tofu, lemon juice, cashews, onion, tomato, salt, soy sauce, apple juice concentrate, turmeric, and nutritional yeast flakes with a small amount of water (¼–½ cup) to desired consistency. Stir in chives and dill weed.

MAKES: 1½ cups

Mystery Dressing

1 cup **toasted wheat germ**
1¼ cup **olive oil**
¼ cup **dark toasted sesame oil**
1 cup **fresh lemon juice**
½ cup **soy sauce**
½ cup **nutritional yeast flakes**
3 garlic **cloves**
1 teaspoon **raw ginger**
½ cup **water**

Toast the wheat germ by spreading evenly out on a cookie sheet and baking at 350 degrees for about 10 minutes, stirring once during baking time. The toasted wheat germ is what gives this dressing the mysterious texture.

Place wheat germ in a blender. Blend until a fine powder. Add olive oil, sesame oil, lemon juice, soy sauce, nutritional yeast flakes, garlic, ginger, and water. Blend until thoroughly emulsified.

MAKES: 3 cups

Cilantro Dressing

⅓ cup **flax seed gel** (p. 108) or oil
¼ cup **chopped fresh cilantro**
⅓ cup **lemon juice**
½ teaspoon **salt**
½ teaspoon **Spike®**

Blend flax seed gel or oil, cilantro, lemon juice, salt, and Spike® for 30–45 seconds. This dressing is good with Barley Corn Salad or greens of your choice.

MAKES: ⅔ cup

Soups

Hearty Lentil Soup

5 cups **water**
1½ cup **green lentils**
1 bay **leaf**
1 cup **diced carrots**
1 cup **chopped onion**
½ cup **chopped celery**
2 minced **garlic cloves**
1½ tablespoons **Chicken-style Seasoning****

½ tablespoon **celery seed**
½ tablespoon **oregano**
½ tablespoon **savory**
1½ tablespoons **lemon juice**
1½ tablespoons **dried parsley**
1 cup **diced tomatoes**
¾ cup **tomato paste**

Put water in a large stockpot over medium heat along with bay leaf. Bring to a boil. Add lentils, returning to a boil and simmer for 20–30 minutes, uncovered.

Sauté carrots, onion, celery, and garlic in a small amount of water or oil until they are tender. Add to lentils. When the lentils are completely done, add Chicken-style Seasoning, celery seed, oregano, savory, lemon juice, parsley, diced tomato and tomato paste. Mix together. Return to a boil and serve.

SERVES: 10

Basic Potato Soup

8 cups **boiling water**
4 or **5 chopped potatoes**
1 medium **chopped onion**
1 teaspoon **Vege-Sal®**

1½ tablespoons **Chicken-style Seasoning****
½ teaspoon **garlic powder**
1 teaspoon **dried parsley**
½ teaspoon **basil**

Sauté the onion in a small amount of water until tender. Add water to make 8 cups and bring to a boil, and then add potatoes. Simmer for 20 minutes or until tender.

Add Vege-Sal®, Chicken-style Seasoning, garlic powder, parsley, and basil once the potatoes are fully cooked. Simmer together for 10 minutes to allow flavors to meld.

SERVES: 10

Potato Corn Chowder

Make the basic "Potato Soup" recipe.
2 cups **frozen corn**
1 cup **raw cashews**

Add frozen corn, return to a boil. Take 1 cup of hot soup broth and blend with raw cashews. Blend on high until very smooth, 1–2 minutes.

Stir blended cashew mixture into the soup, and continue stirring until soup returns to a boil.

SERVES: 10

Vegetable Wild Rice Soup

1 cup **wild rice**
3 cups **water**
2 cups **fresh sliced mushrooms**
½ cup **chopped celery**
½ cup **chopped green pepper**
½ cup **chopped onion**
1 cup **tomato pieces**
6 cups **additional water**
¼ cup **Chicken-style Seasoning*** (p. 64)

Cook rice in water until rice is tender, about 45 minutes.

Sauté mushrooms, celery, pepper, and onion in small amount of water until mushrooms are completely tender. Add to cooked wild rice.

Add tomatoes and seasoning to veggies and rice, simmer and additional 15–20 minutes to blend flavors.

SERVES: 10

Chickpea Tahini Soup

8 cups **water**
6 cups **cooked chickpeas**
⅓ cup **Chicken-style Seasoning** (p. 64)
1 **bay leaf**
¾ tablespoons **cumin**
1 teaspoons **Vege-Sal**®
1 large **garlic cloves**, pressed
1 teaspoon **Spike**®
½ tablespoon **dried dill weed**
2 cup **cabbage**, thinly sliced
3 tablespoons **lemon juice**
5 green **onions**, chopped
½ cup **Tahini**

Pour water into a large stockpot; add cooked chickpeas, Chicken-style Seasoning, bay leaves, cumin, Vege-Sal®, garlic, Spike®, and dill weed in a large stock pot. Simmer to meld flavors.

Add cabbage, lemon juice, and green onions. Return to a simmer before adding Tahini. Return to a simmer and serve.

This is absolutely one of our favorite soups!

SERVES: 10

Multi-Bean Soup

2 cups **assorted dry beans**
1 small **onion**, chopped
1 **green pepper**, chopped
½ cup **celery**, chopped
½ cup **carrots**, diced
1 cup **canned tomatoes**, diced
¼ cup **Chicken-style seasoning**

Place beans in pressure cooker with 16 cups of water. Allow to cook for 1 hour. If you don't want to cook the beans yourself, you can use an assortment of canned beans. When the beans have cooked, and pressure goes down, remove the lid.

Sauté the onions, pepper, celery, and carrots in 1 tablespoon olive oil or water, just until crispy.

Add to beans along with tomatoes and Chicken-style Seasoning. Bring to a slow simmer to meld flavors for 5–10 minutes and serve.

SERVES: 10

Basic Cheese Soup

1 recipe **of Melty Cheese** (3½ cups) (p. 57)
½ cup **Chicken-style Seasoning** (p. 64)
8 cups **water**
12 cups **broccoli or cauliflower**

Prepare Melty Cheese according to the recipe.

Add water and Chicken-style Seasoning. Bring to a simmer. Add the vegetable or vegetables of choice.

SERVES: 10

Quinoa Butternut Soup

3 tablespoons **olive oil or water**
1 small **onions**, chopped
3 large cloves **garlic**, pressed
4 cups **butternut squash**, peeled and diced
1 cup **quinoa**, well rinsed
½ cup **Chicken-style Seasoning** (p. 64)

Sauté the onion, garlic and squash in olive oil or water. Add 8 cups of water and bring to a boil.

Put the quinoa in the boiling water and lower the heat. Cook for 20–25 minutes. Squash and quinoa should be soft in this amount of time. Add Chicken-style Seasoning.

SERVES: 10

Curried Cauliflower Soup

1 tablespoon **olive oil or water**
1 small **onion**, diced fine
2 stalks **celery**, chopped
2 large **potatoes**, diced
6 cups **water**
⅓ cup **Chicken-style Seasoning** (p. 64)

1 teaspoon **curry powder**
½ head **cauliflower**, cut into bite-sized pieces
1 cup **frozen peas**
1 recipe (2½ cups) **Melty Cheese** (p. 57), minus red pepper and the last cup of water.*

Sauté the onions and celery in olive oil or water.

Bring 6 cups water to a boil and add diced potatoes along with sautéed onion and celery. Mix in Chicken-style Seasoning, curry powder, cauliflower, and peas, and bring to a boil.

Make Melty Cheese (p. 57) and add to the simmering soup mixture. Return to a boil. Serve.

SERVES: 10

Split Green Pea Soup

5 cups **water**
1¼ cups **split green peas**
1 large **bay leaf**
1 large **potato or sweet potato**, diced (or both)
1 small **red onion**, diced
1 small **carrot**, diced

½ cup **celery**, diced
¼ cup **Chicken-style Seasoning** (p. 64)
½ teaspoon **curry powder**, optional
¼ teaspoon **granulated garlic**
1½ teaspoons **granulated onion**

Cook split peas in 5 cups water with the bay leaf at a gentle boil for one hour. Add potatoes and continue to cook for 10 minutes.

Sauté the onion, carrot, and celery in a small amount of olive oil or water until veggies are tender. Add to split pea mixture along with Chicken-style Seasoning, curry powder, garlic powder, and onion powder. Bring to a simmer and serve.

*To add another dimension to this soup, add a batch (3½ cups) of Melty Cheese (p. 57).

SERVES: 10

Chickpea & Artichoke Stew

1 large **onion**, chopped
2 garlic **cloves**, pressed
3 large **potatoes**
8 cups **water**
1 frozen **package squash or a small can of pumpkin**
3 cups **cooked chickpeas**
1 teaspoons **turmeric**
1 teaspoons **paprika**
1 teaspoons **rosemary**
½ teaspoon **sage**
1 (14-ounce) can **artichoke hearts**
⅓ cup **Chicken-style Seasoning** (p. 64)
¼ cup **lemon juice**

Sauté onions, garlic, and potatoes in a small amount of olive oil or water until onion is tender.

Add 8 cups of water, squash, chick peas, and turmeric, paprika, rosemary, and sage.

Cook all of the above ingredients together for 20 minutes or until the potatoes are cooked completely. Add the artichoke hearts, Chicken-style Seasoning and very last add the lemon juice. Return to a simmer and serve.

SERVES: 10

Potato, Green Chili Cheese Soup

2 cups **water**
2 **potatoes**, scrubbed and diced
¼ large **onion**, diced fine
1 small **garlic clove**, pressed
3 tablespoons **Chicken-style Seasoning** (p. 64)
½ cup **frozen corn kernels**
2 tablespoons **green chili peppers**
1 teaspoon **chili powder**
1 recipe (**2½ cups**) **Melty Cheese**, minus the last 1 cup of water (p. 57)

Bring water to a boil, add potatoes and cook while you dice the onions and press the garlic. Add the onion and garlic to potatoes along with Chicken-style Seasoning, corn, green chili peppers, and chili powder.

Make your Melty Cheese while the potato mixture cools, remembering to omit the last cup of water.

Pour Melty Cheese into potatoes stirring as you do and return to a boil. Potato soup with zip! Serve it while it's hot!

SERVES: 10

Bread Bowls

Bread bowls are fun to serve homemade soups in, and can be easy to make! Take your favorite basic whole wheat bread recipe, make it up, and divide it into 8-ounce portions. Roll each portion into a large roll. Let rise for 15–20 minutes. Bake at 350 degrees for 20–25 minutes. You will want the outside to be crispy. Once your large "buns" are done, cut the top off and hollow out the inside. Now you're ready to place your favorite soup in the **"Bread Bowls!"**

Sweets (Desserts)

Apple Pie (Contest Winner)

2 **Fuji apples** (peel only one)
2 **Golden Delicious apples** (peel only one)
2 **Granny Smith apples** (peel only one)
½ teaspoon **allspice**
Pinch of **salt**
12 ounces **frozen apple juice concentrate**
2 rounded tablespoons of **cornstarch**

Core all apples and cut into thin slices. (I like to leave some skin on the apples because there are a lot of nutrients just under the skin plus a lot of good fiber.)

Steam apples in ¼ cup water in a large skillet for about 10 minutes, covered. Add allspice, salt and apple juice concentrate to the skillet when apples are soft. Continue to simmer and add the cornstarch that has been dissolved in 2 tablespoons of cold water. Continue to stir until thickened.

Pour into an unbaked pie crust (see recipe below). Top with another crust or crumble topping (recipe to follow).

Crumble topping:

½ cup **old-fashioned oats**
½ cup **flour**
½ cup **Sucanat®**
¼ cup **Earth Balance® Margarine**

Mix together oats, flour, Sucanat®, and margarine, and crumble over the top of the apple pie.

Bake at 350 degrees for 30 minutes. If you use a second crust on top instead of the crumble topping the baking time is the same.

SERVES: 8

Wheat Pie Crust

2 cups **whole wheat flour**, slightly packed
Or whole **wheat pastry flour**, slightly packed

½ teaspoon **salt**
½ cup **water**
½ cup **canola oil**

> **Tips/Comments**
> For a new look and taste, roll finely chopped walnuts into your crust before baking.

Put flours and salt into a bowl.

Whisk oil and water together to emulsify them. Add to dry ingredients.

Mix together until moist and roll out for the type of crust you desire. I like to use two layers of plastic wrap and roll the pie crust between them. It is very pliable, and I can lift it up and see if it is even. If baked alone, prick with fork and bake at 350 degrees for 25 minutes.

MAKES: 2 (9-inch) pie crusts

Mixed Berry Crisp

Crust

1 cup **quick oats**
1 cup **sifted whole wheat pastry flour**
1 cup **finely chopped walnuts**
A pinch of **salt**
¼ cup **Sucanat®**
½ cup **Earth Balance® Margarine**
2 tablespoons **cold water**

Filling

2 pounds of **frozen mixed berries**
1 can of **frozen apple juice concentrate**
¼ cup of **water**
3 tablespoons **corn starch**

Place oats, flour, nuts, salt, Sucanat®, and Earth Balance® in a mixing bowl. Work the Earth Balance® in until it disappears. Add the cold water and mix just enough to hold mixture together.

Press into a 10-inch pie plate.

Bake at 350 degrees for 15 minutes. While it is baking, do the following: Place the berries and apple juice concentrate in a saucepan and thaw on low heat. Mix water and cornstarch together until the cornstarch is dissolved. Pour the cornstarch mixture over the heated berry mixture. Stir continually until thickened.

Pour thickened berry mixture into your baked pie crust (from recipe above). You can reserve a half a cup of crust crumbles to sprinkle over the top of the crisp. Bake for an extra 15 minutes.

SERVES: 8

Sesame Crunch Bars

1½ cups **coconut**
½ cup **maple syrup**
2½ cups **sesame seeds**
1 teaspoon **vanilla**
¼ cup **almond butter or other nut butter**
¾ teaspoon **salt**
½ cup **chopped nuts**
¼ cup **Corn Butter** (p. 59)

Mix coconut, maple syrup, sesame seeds, vanilla nut butter, salt, nuts, and Corn Butter very well.

Press this mixture very firmly into the bottom of a sprayed 9 x 13-inch pan.

Bake mixture at 350 degrees for 30–35 minutes or until nicely browned. Cool, and cut into 24 pieces.

MAKES: 24 bars

Chia Pudding

3–4 tablespoons **chia seeds**
1¾ cups **almond/soy/coconut milk**
½ teaspoon **vanilla**
1 tablespoon **pure maple syrup**

Mix the chia seeds and milk together, stirring as you do to prevent clumping. Add in vanilla and maple syrup.

Place in a container that can be sealed, and stir every few minutes for about a half hour and chill overnight. This method makes a tapioca-like consistency. If you prefer, you can blend all ingredients.

SERVES: 3

Tips/Comments

I find that the amount of chia seeds needed varies from milk to milk. Whole coconut milk needs less chia seed, where almond milk needs a little more. Experiment until you find your perfect balance.

Fig Bars

Crust:
½ cup **flax seed gel** (p. 108) or **oil**
¾ teaspoon **salt**
½ cup **apple juice concentrate** or **honey**
1½ cups **quick oats**
¼ cup **applesauce**
½ cup **walnut pieces** (opt.)
1¾ cups **whole wheat flour**

Fruit Filling:
3 cups **dried fruit (figs or apricots)**
1½ cups **water**

Mix flax seed gel or oil, salt, juice concentrate or honey, oats, applesauce, walnut pieces, and flour. Press ½ of the crust mixture into a sprayed 9x13-inch pan. Reserve the rest of the crust mixture for the top of the bar.

Steam dried fruit and water together until soft. To create a smooth texture, process with the S blade in a food processor. Spread over the crust in the bottom of the pan. Place remaining crust on the fruit filling and press down gently. You can roll out the remaining crust between two pieces of plastic wrap for an even top.

Bake at 400 degrees for 20–25 minutes or until golden brown. Let cool before cutting into 24 pieces.

MAKES: 24 bars

Date Carob Chip Cookies

1 cup **walnuts** or **Brazil nuts**
1 cup **dates**
½ teaspoon **salt**
1½ cup **water**
2 teaspoons **vanilla**
1¼ cups **whole wheat pastry flour**
1 cup **carob chips**
1 cup **raisins**
1 cup **chopped nuts**

Blend the nuts, dates, salt, water, and vanilla. Pour into a bowl and add the flour, carob chips, raisins, and nuts.

Mix all ingredients and drop 2 tablespoons at a time onto a sprayed cookie sheet.

Bake at 350 degrees for 20 minutes.

MAKES: 2 dozen

Carob Pudding #1

2 cups **pitted dates**
1 cup **water**
¼ cup **white grape juice concentrate** or **honey**
30 ounces **extra firm silken tofu**
¼ cup **carob powder**
½ teaspoon **coffee substitute powder** or **granules**
1 tablespoon **vanilla**

Boil dates and water together long enough to soften dates, about 5 minutes.

Put dates, juice concentrate, tofu, carob powder, coffee substitute powder, and vanilla into a blender and blend until very smooth.

Chill and serve with a sprinkle of granola on top.

MAKES: 1½ cups

Carob Pudding #2

2 packages of **silken tofu**
½ cup **honey**
⅓ cup **oil**
2 tablespoons **carob powder**
2 tablespoons **peanut** or **almond butter**

Blend tofu, honey, oil, carob powder, and nut butter until smooth. Refrigerate and serve when chilled.

MAKES: 2½ cups

Flax Seed Gel (Egg substitute)

2 cups **boiling water**
6 tablespoons **flax seeds**

Boil flax seeds in water for 5 minutes. Pour mixture through a wire strainer and catch the gel in a bowl. Discard seeds that remain in the strainer.

YIELD: 1 cup

Some use this mixture for a tea to soothe the intestines, but I like to use it as an oil replacement. Flax seeds are high in omega fatty acids, which boost the immune system and will significantly reduce cholesterol and triglyceride levels.

Flax Egg Replacer

3 tablespoons **ground flax seed**, golden is best
1 tablespoon **oil**, your choice
¾ cup **hot water**

Place flax, oil and water in a blender, blender bullet works best, and blend for one minute. 1/4 cup will replace 1 egg. This mixture has the binding ability of an egg but does not expand the same way an egg will.

Raisin Ball Cookies

3/4 cup **white grape juice concentrate or honey**
1 cup **ground raisins**
1/2 cup **Corn Butter** (p. 59)
3 cups **whole wheat pastry flour**
⅓ cup **oil**
⅛ teaspoon **salt**
¼ cup **applesauce**
½ cup **chopped walnuts**
1 teaspoon **vanilla**

Mix juice concentrate or honey, raisins, Corn Butter, flour, oil, salt, applesauce, walnuts, and vanilla together. Roll into 1-inch balls.

Bake at 350 degrees for 10–15 minutes.

MAKES: 2 dozen

> **Tips/Comments**
> Tip: I find it hard to grind the raisins without adding some of the flour in with the raisins. This keeps the raisins from sticking together.

Raisin Bars

2 cups **raisins**
1 cup **Corn Butter** (p. 59) or oil
1⅓ cups **old-fashioned oats**
½ cup **white grape juice concentrate or honey**
1¾ cups **whole wheat pastry flour**
¾ cup **flax seed gel**
1 cup **Tofu Sour Cream** (p. 61)
½ cup **white grape juice concentrate or honey**
2½ tablespoons **cornstarch**
1 teaspoon **vanilla**

Cook raisins in ½-1 cup water for 10 minutes. Drain off extra water.

Cream Corn Butter. Mix oats, juice or honey, and flour together. Press half of mixture into 9 x 13-inch pan.

Bake at 350 degrees for 7 minutes.

Mix the flax seed gel, Tofu Sour Cream, juice or honey, and cornstarch. Stir and boil until thick. Add raisins and vanilla. Pour over a baked crust. Crumble rest of the oatmeal mixture over raisins.

Bake for 30 minutes at 350 degrees. Cut and serve.

MAKES: 24 bars

Carob Snowballs

1 cup **dates**
¼ cup **water**
3 tablespoons **nut butter (almond, peanut, etc.)**
½ cup **carob chips**
1 teaspoon **coffee substitute powder or granules**
½ cup **raisins**
¼ cup **chopped dried pineapple**
½ teaspoon **salt**
1 cup **chopped nuts**
1½ teaspoon **vanilla**
1 teaspoon **citrus peel**
1 teaspoon **carob powder**
⅓ cup **sunflower seeds**
1 cup **Grape-Nuts®**

Simmer dates and water together until water is absorbed. Stir in nut butter with dates mixture while it is still warm to help the nut butter dissolve.

Mix carob chips, dried pineapple, salt, nuts, vanilla, citrus peel, carob powder, sunflower seeds well. Add Grape-Nuts®, and mix well with other ingredients.

Form into balls and roll in coconut if desired. These are messy to make but delicious.

MAKES: 24

Coconut Pie Crust

¾ cup **coconut**
1 cup **Grape-Nuts®**
2–3 tablespoons **white grape juice concentrate**

Blend coconut and Grape-Nuts®. Stir in juice. Press into pie plate.

Bake at 350 degrees for 15 minutes.

MAKES: 1 pie crust

No Bake Pumpkin Pie

¼ cup **cashews**
1½ cups **warm water**
3 tablespoons **kosher gelatin**
1 teaspoon **vanilla**

¼ cup **Sucanat®**
¼ cup **maple syrup**
¾ teaspoon **salt**
1 (15-ounce) **can pumpkin,** add last

Blend cashews in warm water, gelatin, vanilla, Sucanat®, maple syrup, and salt thoroughly, adding pumpkin gradually after nuts are well blended and adding more water if needed.

Pour into a pre-baked pie crust. Garnish with pecan halves or a sprinkle of coconut. Chill and serve.

MAKES: 1 pie

Oatmeal Raisin Cookies

½ cup **flax seed gel** (p. 108) or oil
¼ cup **applesauce**
1 cup **apple juice concentrate or honey**
1 teaspoon **vanilla**
1 cup **whole wheat pastry flour**

1 teaspoon **salt**
1 teaspoon **coriander or cinnamon**
1 cup **raisins**
¾ cup **chopped walnuts**
3 cups **oats** (can be ½ thick and ½ thin)

Blend flax seed gel or oil, applesauce, apple juice or honey, and vanilla together. If you are using flax seed gel, you will want to do this in the blender. Put into a medium-sized bowl.

Mix flour, salt, coriander or cinnamon, raisins, walnuts, and oats into the bowl with the wet ingredients. Combine all ingredients together.

Form into cookies, place on baking sheet.

Bake at 350 degrees for 15–20 minutes.

MAKES: 18

South Dakota Pecan Pie

1 cup **dates**
2 cups **water or flax seed gel** (p. 108)
1 tablespoon **nut butter (almond, peanut)**
¼ teaspoon **salt** (opt.)
¼ cup **cornstarch mixed in 1 cup cold water**

1 teaspoon **vanilla**
2 tablespoons **maple syrup**
1 teaspoon **carob powder (optional)**
1 cup **pecans**

Simmer the dates in a saucepan with water or flax seed gel. When dates are well softened, blend in blender until smooth. Add nut butter, salt, and the cornstarch mixed in cold water. Return to pan and continue to simmer to desired thickness then add vanilla, maple syrup, and carob powder.

Mix in one cup of pecans. Pour into an unbaked pie crust, cover filling with a layer of pecans brushed with maple syrup. (Flaky Wheat-Oat Crust on page 12 goes very well with this recipe.)

Bake at 350 degrees or until the crust is nicely browned, about 40 minutes.

MAKES: 1 pie

> **Tips/Comments**
> This pie was dreamed up while we lived in South Dakota, thus the name.

Pecan Pie

Preheat oven to 350 degrees

1¼ cups **flax seed gel** (p. 108) (one batch)
1 tablespoon **Earth Balance® Margarine**
⅓ cup **honey**
⅔ cup **Sucanat® or brown sugar**
¾ cup **water**
2 teaspoons **cornstarch**

1 teaspoon **vanilla**
1 teaspoon **aluminum-free baking powder**
⅛ teaspoon **salt**
½ to 1 cup **chopped pecans**
24 **pecan halves**
1 **Wheat Pie Crust** (p. 105)

Beat the flax seed gel with an egg beater till it is foamy and then add melted margarine, honey, Sucanat®, water, corn starch, vanilla, and baking powder. Beat mixture again to dissolve Sucanat®.

Fold in salt and pecan pieces. Pour into pie crust and place pecan halves on top.

Bake for approximately 30 minutes or until crust and filling are golden brown.

MAKES: 1 pie

Baked Sopaipillas (sok-paee-peeyas)

(Mexican Dessert)

1¼ cups **warm cashew milk** (110 degrees)
1¼ tablespoons **yeast**
⅓ cup **honey**
¼ cup **Corn Butter** (p. 59)
1 teaspoon **salt**

2 cups **whole wheat flour**
2 cups **unbleached flour**
¼ cup **Sucanat® or brown sugar**
1 teaspoon **coriander or cinnamon**

Heat cashew milk until bath water warm (110 degrees) in a small saucepan and place in a large bowl. (If milk is too hot, it will kill the yeast.) Add honey and yeast, mix until yeast is dissolved. Allow to get foamy. After the liquid mixture is foamy, add 2–3 tablespoons of the Corn Butter, the flours (saving ½–1 cup back to add in as needed while kneading), and salt.

Knead for 10 to 15 minutes by hand to mix well. The dough should be soft but not sticking to your hands. Roll out dough in a square until it is about ½-inch thick. Cut in squares of desired size, and place on sprayed cookie sheet. Leave space between each one for growth. Let rise for 20 minutes, in a warm place.

Bake in a very hot oven, 450 degrees, for 15 minutes or until golden brown. Brush with remaining Corn Butter and sprinkle with Sucanat® (or brown sugar) and coriander mixture.

Sopaipillas are traditionally served with a bit of honey to dip them in.

MAKES: 12

White Tofu Cheesecake (Granola Crust)

Step One: Crust

3 cups **Granola** (p. 8)
2 tablespoons **applesauce**
1 tablespoon **white grape juice concentrate**

Step Two: Filling

36 ounces **extra firm silken tofu**
¼ teaspoon **almond extract**
3 tablespoons **lemon juice**
1 tablespoon **vanilla extract**
½ cup **white grape juice concentrate**

½ cup **honey**
2 tablespoons **cornstarch**

Step three: Glaze Topping

2 tablespoons **cornstarch**
2 cups **frozen fruit**
1 cup **apple juice concentrate**

Crust: Blend Granola until fine. Pour into a mixing bowl. Add applesauce and juice concentrate to Granola and mix together until all of the Granola is moist. Pack mixture tightly into pan. A nine-inch spring form pan works great! Set aside and go to step two.

Filling: Place tofu, almond extract, lemon juice, vanilla extract, juice concentrate, honey, and cornstarch into a blender and blend well on high. Pour over crust and bake at 350 degrees for 35 minutes. Best if refrigerated overnight before proceeding to step three (Glaze Topping). You can use this for a pudding by leaving out the cornstarch.

Glaze Topping: For a blended glaze topping, place cornstarch, fruit, and juice concentrate into a blender and blend on high until smooth. For a topping with the fruit intact, blend only the juice concentrate and cornstarch together. Pour mixture into a small skillet and heat over medium heat. Stir continually until mixture thickens. Immediately pour over cooled cheesecake. Let topping set up for at least an hour in the refrigerator. Cut and serve.

MAKES: 1 cheesecake

Alternate Cheesecake Filling
Carob Tofu Cheesecake

2 cups **pitted dates**
1 cup **water**
3 (12.3 ounce aseptic packaging) **bricks extra firm silken tofu**
1 teaspoon **coffee substitute powder, such as Cafix®**
1 teaspoon **vanilla**
¼ cup **carob powder**
¼ cup **honey**
½ cup **milk substitute**, such as soy
2 teaspoons **cornstarch**

Boil 1 cup water and dates together for 5 minutes to soften dates. Once the dates are soft, place them along with the tofu, coffee substitute powder, vanilla, carob powder, honey, milk, and cornstarch into a blender, and blend until everything is silky smooth. Pour over Granola Crust.

Bake for 35 minutes at 350 degrees.

Best if refrigerated overnight before proceeding to step three (Glaze Topping above). You can use this for a pudding by leaving out the cornstarch.

Coconut Frosting

1 cup **white grape juice concentrate**
½ cup **water**
2 tablespoons **cornstarch** mixed with 2 tablespoons cold water
1 cup **coconut**, toasted
1 cup **nuts**, chopped and toasted
½ teaspoon **salt**

Bring sweetener and ½ cup water to a boil and add the cornstarch mixed with cold water and stir until mixture thickens. You may toast coconut and chopped nuts together in the oven at 350 degrees for 15 minutes, stirring often.

Remove the sweet mixture from the heat and add salt, toasted coconut, and toasted nuts. Mix together. Spread on your favorite cake.

This is a great frosting for Carob Cake (p. 118)!

Maple Nut Ice Cream

½ cup **chopped dates**
3 tablespoons **maple syrup**
2 cups **coconut milk**

¾ cup **chopped pecans**
Pinch of **salt**

Blend the dates, maple syrup, and coconut milk.

Pour into your ice cream freezer and freeze, and then add pecans.

MAKES: 3 cups

Easy Pie Crust

1 cup **Grape-Nuts**®
1 cup **raw nuts**
2 tablespoons **fruit juice or honey**

Blend Grape-Nuts and nuts together in a dry blender. Stir in fruit juice concentrate (white grape) or honey. Mix together until nicely blended.

Press lightly into a 9-inch pie plate.

Bake at 350 degrees, until lightly browned, about 15 minutes. This resembles a graham cracker crust and can be used in the same way.

MAKES: 1 pie crust

Rich Carob Pie

1 cup **raw cashews**
1½ cups **chopped dates**
1 tablespoon **coffee substitute powder or granules (Roma® is my favorite)**
½ teaspoon **salt**
1½ teaspoons **vanilla**
¼ cup **carob powder**
⅓ cup **cornstarch**

Blend cashews, dates, coffee substitute powder, salt, vanilla, and carob powder while gradually adding 4 cups warm water; blend thoroughly (a couple of minutes). Blend in cornstarch.

Thicken over medium heat in a heavy saucepan. While your pudding is heating, stir constantly with a whisk. Pour into pre-baked pie crust. Chill until set. Best if left overnight.

MAKES: 1 pie

Spice Cake

2 cups **sifted whole wheat pastry flour**
¼ cup **unbleached flour**
1 teaspoon **coriander**
½ teaspoon **allspice**
½ teaspoon **salt**
¼ teaspoon **cardamom**

⅔ cup **soy milk**
½ cup **flax seed gel** (p. 108) or **oil**
½ cup **white grape juice concentrate** or **honey**
1 teaspoon **vanilla**
⅓ cup **3% hydrogen peroxide** or 2 teaspoons **aluminum-free baking powder**

Sift together the flours, coriander, allspice, salt, and cardamom in a medium sized bowl.

Blend flax seed gel or oil, juice concentrate, soy milk, and vanilla together for 20–30 seconds.

Fold into the flour mixture and beat with an electric mixer for 2–3 minutes. Last, fold in hydrogen peroxide or baking powder, gently but quickly.

Pour batter into two sprayed 8x8-inch pans or round cake pans. It is better to have two thin layers than one thick layer because vegan cakes tend to be moister and it makes you think they are still raw.

Bake at 350 degrees for 30 minutes.

MAKES: 1 (8x8) cake

Almond Butter Bites

1 cup **almond butter**
3 tablespoons **honey or jelly**
2 tablespoons **flour (whole wheat, oat, rice)**
6 tablespoons **rice crispy cereal or granola**

Stir the almond butter, honey or jelly and flour together until nicely mixed. Stir in rice crispy cereal or granola, form into balls and roll in extra rice crispy cereal, granola or coconut (your choice). These can become Peanut Butter Bites by substituting peanut butter for almond butter.

You can melt chocolate and drizzle over each ball. Chopped nuts would be a good addition to this recipe.

MAKES: 24

Carob Brownies

⅔ cup **Earth Balance® margarine**
1 cup **hot water**
¼ cup **flax meal**
1 teaspoon **vanilla**
4 tablespoons **carob powder**

2 cups **Sucanat®** (p. 116)
1¼ cups **whole wheat pastry flour**
1 teaspoon **aluminum-free baking powder**
1 teaspoon **salt**
1 cup **chopped walnuts**

Preheat oven to 350 degrees. Grease and flour a 9 x 13-inch baking pan.

Melt margarine and blend with hot water and flax meal to make a foamy mixture. Add vanilla to this mixture.

Mix carob, Sucanat®, flour, baking powder, salt, and nuts together in a medium sized bowl. Now add water mixture and stir well. Spread in floured pan.

Bake 30 minutes or until brownies start to pull away from the sides of the pan. Cool before cutting in 2 x 1½-inch squares.

MAKES: 18

Carob Cake

2 cups **sifted whole wheat pastry flour**
1 tablespoon **coffee substitute powder or granules**
¼ cup **carob powder**
½ teaspoon **salt**
½ cup **flax seed gel** (p. 108) or **oil**
¾ cup **soy milk**
½ cup **white grape juice concentrate** or **honey**
1 teaspoon **vanilla**
⅓ cup **3% hydrogen peroxide** or 2 teaspoons **aluminum-free baking powder**

Combine flour, coffee substitute powder, carob powder, and salt in a medium bowl until nicely mixed. In a large bowl, combine flax seed gel or oil, soy milk, juice concentrate or honey, and vanilla and mix well.

Add dry ingredients to wet and whip for a few minutes to remove lumps. Stir in hydrogen peroxide or baking powder, gently but quickly.

Pour batter into two sprayed 8x8-inch pans. It is better to have two thin layers than one thick layer because vegan cakes tend to be moister and it makes you think they are still raw.

Bake at 350 degrees for 30 minutes.

MAKES: 1 (8x8) cake

> **Tips/Comments**
>
> When using hydrogen peroxide, don't be surprised if it has a "bleaching" effect on your other ingredients. The consumption of baking soda and baking powder inhibits the digestive process. As an alternative, you can use hydrogen peroxide, which is H_2O_2. In the baking process, the second oxygen is cooked off, leaving water.

Carob Chip Cookies

4 cups **sifted whole wheat pastry flour**
1 teaspoon **salt**
1 tablespoon **aluminum-free baking powder**
¾ cup **walnuts**, chopped
1 cup **carob chips**
¾ cup **oil**
1 cup **honey**
¾ cup **applesauce**
2 teaspoons **vanilla**

Mix flour, salt, baking powder, nuts and carob chips in a large bowl. Mix together oil, honey, applesauce, and vanilla.

Fold liquids into dry ingredients until nicely mixed. **Do not over mix.**

Place scoops of cookie dough onto baking sheet. Press down to flatten.

Bake at 350 degrees for 15 minutes.

MAKES: 24

Cream Cheese Frosting

8 ounces **Tofutti® Better Than Cream Cheese**
½ cup **Earth Balance® Margarine**
⅓ cup **Vanilla Soy Milk Powder**
Dash of **salt**
¼ cup **honey**
1 tablespoon **vanilla**

Combine cream cheese, margarine, soy milk powder, salt, honey, and vanilla in a food processor. Process until very smooth, light and fluffy. Tastes great on Carrot Cake!

MAKES: 1½ cups

Lemon Poppy Seed Cookies

4½ cups **sifted whole wheat pastry flour**
1 teaspoon **salt**
1 tablespoon **aluminum-free baking powder**
3 tablespoons **poppy seeds**
¼ cup **lemon juice**
¾ cup **oil**
1 cup **honey**
¾ cup **applesauce**
2 teaspoons **vanilla**

Mix flour, salt, baking powder, and poppy seeds in a large bowl. Mix together lemon juice, oil, honey, applesauce, and vanilla.

Fold the mixed liquid ingredients into the dry ingredients until nicely mixed. **Do not over mix.**

Place scoops of cookie dough onto baking sheet. Press down.

Bake at 350 degrees for 12 minutes.

MAKES: 18

Savory Honey Basil Lemonade

8 cups **water**
6 **lemons**, juiced
½ cup **honey**
4 (4-leaf) sections of **fresh basil**

Stir water, lemon juice, honey, and basil together, and add ice if desired.

Crush the basil leaves to bring out the basil flavor. Serve.

Index

Glossary

Bragg Liquid Aminos®: A non-fermented soy sauce that can be used as a seasoning.

Couscous: Fast cooking spherical semolina wheat that can be used in the place of rice.

Earth Balance® Natural Buttery Spread: Dairy free buttery spread rich in Omega 3's.

Instant Coffee Substitute: A non-coffee drink such as *Postum®*, *Cafix®*, *Inka®*, *Roma®*, *Pero®*, and *Teeccino®*

Kosher Gelatin: guar gum and carrageenan product made primarily from agar agar.

Nutritional Yeast Flakes: An enhancing flavor that is high in B-complex vitamins & protein.

Pizza Seasoning: A perfect spice for pizza and other Italian foods. We prefer the *Frontier Herbs®* mixture.

Quinoa: Ancient grain-like seed, about the size and color of millet, which is high in protein.

Refried Beans: We use *Fantastic Foods®* brand of dried seasoned refried beans mix.

Spike®: A flavor seasoning salt with herbs to enhance the flavor of a recipe.

Sucanat®: Acronym for Sugar Cane Natural. Pure dried sugar cane juice.

Tofutti® Better Than Cream Cheese®: Dairy-free cream cheese product.

Tofutti® Better Than Sour Cheese®: Dairy-free sour cream product.

Vege-Sal®: Vegetized Seasoning Salt.

Vegenaise®: Dairy free mayonnaise.

Vitasoy® Soymilk: *Vitasoy®* is a brand of soy milk drinks.

Index

A

Almond Butter Bites 117
Almond Butter Carob Chip Muffins 21
Almond Crackers 27
Almond Milk 10
Apple Glaze 13
Apple Pie 104
Asparagus Bruschetta 74
Autumn Salad 85
Avocado Pasta Salad 86

B

Baked Sopaipillas 113
Baked Tofu 2 43
Banana French Toast 14
Banana Muffins 22
Barley, Corn, & Pepper Salad 81
Basic Bagel Recipe 10
Basic Cheese Soup 99
Basic Muffins (or fruit) 20
Basic Oat Burgers 32
Basic Potato Soup 96
Bean Burgers 33
Berry Crunch 11
"Berry" Good Jam 16
Black Bean Medley 30
Brazil Nut Gravy 43, 61
Bread Bowls 102
Breading Meal 65
Bread Loaf 27
Breakfast Banana Split 17

C

Cajun Style Polenta 73
Calico Corn 70
California Tofu 12
Carob Brownies 117
Carob Cake 118
Carob Chip Cookies 118
Carob "Hot Fudge" Topping 17
Carob Pie 116
Carob Pudding #1 108
Carob Pudding #2 108
Carob Snowballs 110
Carob Tofu Cheesecake 114
Carrot and Nut Coleslaw 87
Carrot Salad 81
Cashew Cheese 37
Cashew Gravy 61
Cashew Jack Cheese 36
Cauliflower Pea Salad 88
Cheesecake 113, 114
"Cheesy" Dijon Salad Dressing 92
Chia Pudding 106
Chicken-style Seasoning 64
Chickpea A La King 49
Chickpea & Artichoke Stew 101
Chickpea Burgers 33
Chickpea Tahini Soup 98
Chili Seasoning 64
Cilantro Dressing 81, 93
Coconut Frosting 115
Coconut Pie Crust 110
Corn Bread 22
Corn Butter 59
Country-Style Seasoning 64
Cream Cheese Frosting 119
Creamy Garlic Salad Dressing 90
Creamy Herb Schmear 56
Creamy Ranch Dressing 90
Creamy Sweet Schmear 12
Creamy Sweet Topping 14
Creamy Tofu Cottage Cheese 82
Crunchy Granola 8
Curried Cauliflower Soup 100

D

Date Butter 60
Date Carob Chip Cookies 107
Date Paste 24
Delicious Oatmeal 17
Dextrinized Brown Rice 43

E

Easy Pie Crust 115
Egg Substitute 62
Ensenada Casserole 47
Ezekiel 4:9 Bread 24

F

Falafel 34
Fig Bars 107
Flaky Wheat-Oat Crust 12
Flax Crackers 28
Flax Egg Replacer 109
Flax Seed Gel 108
For the Birds Salad 85
French Dressing 90
Fresh Whole Fruit 8
Fried Rice 69
Fruit Delight 14
Fruit Pizza 13

G

Garlic Dressing 83
Garlic Ginger Coleslaw 84
Garlic/Oregano Sweet Potatoes 71
Glaze Topping 114
Gluten Steaks 51
Granola Crust 113
Greek "Feta" Salad 78
Greek "Feta" Salad Dressing 91
Greek Green Beans 69
Green Bean Bundles 75
Green Enchiladas 52
Guacamole 57

H

Harvest Nut Roast 46, 51
Hash Brown Waffles 15
Hearty Lentil Soup 96
Honey Granola 9
Honey Lemon Marinade 91
Hummus 56
Hunan 40

I

Instructions for making "Feta." 86
Italian Sauce 36

K

Kale with Tomatoes 68
Ketchup 60

L

Lasagna 35
Leafy Green Fruit Salad 79
Lemon Poppy Seed Cookies 119
Lentil Soup 96

M

Macaroni and Cheese 58
Maple Nut Ice Cream 115
Mazidra 39
Melty Cheese 57
Mexican Lasagna 35
Mild Chili Seasoning 64
Mixed Berry Crisp 105
Multi-Bean Soup 99
Mystery Dressing 92

N

No Bake Pumpkin Pie 111

O

Oatmeal Raisin Cookies 111
Oat Waffles #1 14

Oat Waffles #2 18
Oriental Sauce 42

P

Papaya Trail Mix 62
Parmesan-Like Topping 65
Pasta with Collard Greens 44
Pasta with White Beans 44
Peanut Butter Pasta 40
Peanut Butter Sauce 40
Pecan Pie 111, 112
Pecan Tofu Balls 46
Pesto 66
Pesto Pasta Salad 87
Pizza Seasoning 122
"Poo Butter" 16
Potato Corn Chowder 97
Potato, Green Chili Cheese Soup 101
Potato Patties 36
Potato Soup 96
Pumpkin Pie 111

Q

Quinoa Butternut Soup 99
Quinoa Loaf 53
Quinoa Risotto 38
Quinoa Salad 83

R

Racy Ketchup 60
Raisin Ball Cookies 109
Raisin Bars 109
Ratatouille 48
Red Tip Lettuce Salad 79
Rich Carob Pie 116
Roasted Root Vegetables 72
Royal Coleslaw 89

S

Salsa 56
Sautéed Mushrooms 40
Savory Broth 51
Savory Honey Basil Lemonade 119
Scalloped Potatoes 73
Scrambled Tofu 15
Sesame Crunch Bars 106
Slicing Cheese 58
Smoothies 10
Soft Yellow Cheese-Like Spread 58
South Dakota Pecan Pie 112
Spanish Rice 71
Spelt Bread 25
Spice Cake 116
Spicy Southern Pasta 88
Spinach/Fennel Yams 72
Spinach with Tofu 70
Split Green Pea Soup 100
Spring Pasta Salad 86
Spring Rolls 31
Sprouting 78
Sprout Salad 82
Stir Fry 42
Stroganoff 31, 43
Succotash 45
Summer Vegetable Casserole 42
Super Waffles 18
Sweet Chile Sauce 32, 66

T

Taco Salad Bowls 79
Tahini Blue Cheese Dressing 91
Tamale Pie 39
Tasty Cereal Loaf 48
Tasty "Cheese" Enchiladas 37
Ten Layer Bean Salad 80
The Fajitas Meal 41
Toasted Sunflower Seeds 61
Tofu Mayonnaise 60
Tofu Sour Cream 61
Tofu Yung Patties 50
Twice-baked Potatoes 68

V

Vegan Ricotta 59, 86
Vegetable Wild Rice Soup 97
Volcanos 38

W

Walnut Parmesan Cheese 38, 65
Wheat Pie Crust 105
Whipped Topping 15, 16
White Tofu Cheesecake 113
Whole Wheat Buns 26
Whole Wheat Crepes 9
Whole Wheat Sweet Rolls 23
Whole Wheat Tortillas 28
Wild Rice Casserole 45
Wild Rice Salad 82
Wild Rice Soup 97
Wild Rice Stir Fry 50

Z

Zucchini Muffins 21

Flavor each day with:

      Fruits

      Legumes

      Almonds and other nuts

      Veggies

      Oats and other grains along with

      Rice

                Flavor!

We invite you to view the complete
selection of titles we publish at:
www.TEACHServices.com

We encourage you to write us
with your thoughts about this,
or any other book we publish at:
info@TEACHServices.com

TEACH Services' titles may be purchased in
bulk quantities for educational, fund-raising,
business, or promotional use.
bulksales@TEACHServices.com

Finally, if you are interested in seeing
your own book in print, please contact us at:
publishing@TEACHServices.com

We are happy to review your manuscript at no charge.

www.ingramcontent.com/pod-product-compliance
Lightning Source LLC
Chambersburg PA
CBHW040927240426
43667CB00024B/2978